THE KINGDOM BENEATH THE WELL

M.D. COUTURIER

ISBN: 1517214874
ISBN-13: 978-1517214876

For Tom & Roberta Couturier

CHAPTER ONE
CHRISTINA AND THE ENCHANTED WELL

The moment she heard the last bell ring, Christina jumped up from her desk. She shoved her books into her purple schoolbag, grabbed her jacket, and ran out of the classroom. The day had been awful, as usual. To endure the misery of sixth grade, Christina often imagined that she was a hero locked in a dungeon by a cruel and powerful king who tortured her in an attempt to break her spirit.

Walking down the crowded hallway to her locker, she spotted a group of girls talking. One of them was Sylvia Mack, her best friend in elementary school. She and Christina used to sit together in class and sleep over at each other's houses, but that all ended when they entered middle school. Sylvia started hanging out with the popular girls and avoiding her. Of course, she couldn't afford to be seen with that "weird" Christina who read fairy tales and fantasy novels in the library while the other kids played sports or gossiped about stupid stuff during lunch period. That would hurt Sylvia's chances of acquiring the "right" friends and winning those inane popularity contests more commonly called student council elections.

As Christina approached the girls, they stopped talking and stared at her. With her slight build, blue eyes, and long brown hair, she looked rather pretty. Nevertheless, under the hostile gaze of her peers, Christina felt intensely conscious of her appearance. Pointing at her, one of the girls whispered something to the others, and they all burst out laughing. Christina's face burned, but she responded to her tormentors with stony silence.

After she finally exited the red brick, two-story school building—which always seemed more like a prison to her rather than a place of learning—Christina sped home on her bike. Reaching the end of her driveway, she stopped and stared forlornly at the houses in her neighborhood standing shoulder to shoulder, with their manicured lawns, paved driveways, and two-door garages. Her boring middle-class suburb in Grand Rapids, Michigan was a constant misery, and she longed to travel to a magical world like the ones she always read about in books.

At home, Christina ate some graham crackers before tackling her math assignment. Fractions again. She groaned. After ten minutes of waging a dispirited war against the monster of equations, she slammed her math book shut and bolted upstairs to get her knight costume and plastic sword from her room. Christina then hopped on her bike and pedaled to a glade that lay in the woods beyond the park. Upon reaching it, she quickly dismounted and donned her costume over her jeans and yellow blouse. Surrounded by tall oaks and blanketed with a golden carpet of dandelions, the glade seemed enchanting to her, like something out of a fairy tale.

Christina entered a make-believe world of magic and chivalry, and for the next few hours, this unhappy girl was King Arthur fighting Mordred across the fields of Camlann and Aragorn leading the armies of Gondor in the battle for Middle-Earth. The pitiful screams of the wounded and the sound of metal clanging against metal filled the air as legions of soldiers swept the battlefield around her. In the midst of her imaginary adventures, Christina thought about her father, who had often played with her in the glade before the divorce. Her heart ached as she recalled the time he wore a round black bucket with eyeholes cut into it in order to portray an evil knight.

As darkness approached, she left the woods and pedaled slowly, delaying her return home for as long as possible.

***

Once she arrived at the house, Christina found her mother waiting.

"Christina Marie Janssen!" Mom shouted as her daughter stepped into the foyer. "You left the door unlocked again! How many times have I told you to lock it when you go out? We could have been robbed!"

"I just forgot," Christina said. "Don't freak out about it, *Angela*."

She often called Mom by her first name just to irritate her.

"Stop with the 'Angela' business! I'm your mother, as much as you may hate that! You *always* forget to do things! You never listen to anything I say!"

Christina glowered, but gave no reply.

"Get upstairs," Mom said. "You're grounded for a month. No TV and no going to the woods."

"That's not fair!"

"Oh yes it is! Do what I say and you won't get in trouble."

As Christina turned and trudged to the stairs, she muttered a word under her breath.

"What did you say?" Mom asked in that soft tone which usually signaled danger.

"Nothing."

"It better have been nothing!"

Christina felt a flash of anger, and she whirled around.

"I hate living with you and I hate this place!" she shouted. "I wish I was with Dad! He was always nice to me! He wasn't mean like you!"

"I'm sorry I can't treat you like a queen and give you whatever you desire," Mom said sarcastically. "But somebody has to discipline you! Your father spoiled you rotten and turned you against me!"

"I'm *not* spoiled! And you don't really care about me! You just pretend to! But when I ask for something that means a lot to me, you always say no! Why can't I spend summers at the horse ranch anymore? I did when Dad was around!"

"I can't afford it! Besides, I don't think you deserve to go, given the way you've been acting!"

"You're an awful mom!" Christina yelled. "Dad was a much better parent than you!"

"Oh, really?" Mom replied, her face emblazoned with fury. "Well let me tell you something, young lady! Your father was a selfish pig of a man who cheated on his wife and walked out on his daughter!"

"That's not true!" Christina shouted. "You're the real reason he left! Daddy was right! You are a—"

As the word came out, Christina knew she shouldn't have said it.

Mom raised her hand and slapped Christina in the face, and she reeled slightly. Turning her back to her daughter, Mom said in a soft, hoarse voice, "Just go to your room."

A sulky Christina did as she was told, but when she reached the landing at the top of the stairs, she turned around and shouted, "I hate you, and I wish I never had to see you again!"

Then she stalked to her room and slammed the door. After deciding that she couldn't stay in this house any longer, Christina sat on her bed and stared at a bookcase full of fairy tales and fantasy novels as a plan formed in her mind. She would leave as soon as Mom was asleep and go to Dad's place in California. After the divorce, he had said that he would be too busy to take care of her, but, surely, he would change his mind when he saw how Mom's cruelty had driven Christina away.

***

Christina waited an hour after Mom had gone to bed before acting on her plan. When the time came, she stuffed some clothes, food, and water bottles in her schoolbag and snuck out of the house. The chilly spring air stung her face as she biked out of her neighborhood feeling elated. But after a while, her mind clearing, she realized that she couldn't go to California all by herself without any money. Besides, her father would probably just send her back. Maybe

Mom was right; maybe he was living with another woman.

Christina felt trapped in limbo. She was unable to go forward and unwilling to go back. Returning to her dreadful life was out of the question, and she lacked the courage to face Mom after the horrible things she had said. She decided to go to her special glade and think things over.

When she reached the glade, Christina was shocked to see a round well in the moonlight. Made of gray stone and standing about four feet above the ground, it resembled the ones she often read about in fairy tales. Intrigued, she dismounted from her bike and walked toward it. Looking down into the well, she discovered that it was nearly full to the brim with clear golden water. This was strange, for water usually collects at the bottom of wells.

As Christina stared into the well, the water began swirling rapidly, and she backed away in fright. Suddenly, she felt an invisible force pulling her toward the well; it was as though she were caught in a windstorm whose currents prevented her from reaching safety. As an overwhelming panic set in, Christina struggled and cried out for help, but her efforts were in vain. Nobody came to her aid, and she soon went headfirst into the water with a great *splash*!

A moment later, the well vanished, and the glade looked as though nothing strange had just occurred.

CHAPTER TWO
THE QUEST

Christina discovered that she could breathe in the enchanted water, but this provided little relief as she hurtled toward an unknown destination. She screamed and tried to grab hold of something, but her fingers found only more water. After several terrifying minutes, a faint light appeared below, and she shut her eyes. For a moment, she felt herself flying through air, and then *Ploush!* She landed on something that felt like a giant waterbed.

***

When Christina opened her eyes and sat up, she noticed that her clothes were still dry. Looking around, she found herself in a spacious, round, and empty room. The wall consisted of transparent gemstones that emitted a soft white light, and she could see her face reflected in each gem. Oddly, the reflections showed her frowning, even though she wasn't doing this. Both the floor and the ceiling consisted of the golden water that had carried her to this strange room.

Upon standing, she looked down into the water but couldn't see the bottom. Despite moving about, Christina remained on the surface of this enchanted floor, with each footstep creating a giant ripple. Laughing, she tramped around the room and enjoyed the feeling of walking on water. After tiring of this activity, she went over to the wall, placed her hands across the smooth stones, and gazed at her many reflections. She tried to make the frowns disappear by smiling and contorting her face into funny shapes, but nothing worked. After a few minutes, she ran back to the center of the pool, a trail of ripples following in her wake.

"Hello?" she called out. "Is anyone here?"

As if in reply, a translucent silver being shot out of the wall before her. Christina screamed and nearly fell backwards. Amazed, she stared up at the being hovering five feet in the air. It possessed a head that looked much too large for the rest of its gangling body, and the face had glittering yellow eyes, a majestic beard, and a mouth and nose that looked as though chiseled out of fine stone.

The being looked down at her with a smile and said, "Welcome. My name is Boriandar, and I've been searching a long time for someone like you."

"What are you?" Christina asked in a timid voice.

"I'm a wellwight." He waved his arms around as he spoke, and Christina heard the clinking of chains but saw no manacles on his body.

"Oh," she replied, then asked, "Where am I?"

"You're in the Room Between the Worlds."

"It's a great place you've got here."

"Of course you would think that because you've only arrived," Boriandar said with a dismissive wave of his hand. "But spend thousands of years in this room like I have and you'll discover that it's not so great after all."

"Why have you been here that long?"

"I'm Keeper of the Well of Rulers. It consists of two portals, and so far you've gone through one of them. The second portal lies beneath your feet."

"Can't you leave?"

"No, and here's why." Boriandar shook his arms, and Christina once again heard the sound of chains rattling. "I was once a free wellwight and went wherever I pleased. Then one day a sorcerer named Ethindir came along and offered me a great deal of power, and I accepted without hesitation like a greedy fool. He took me down the Well, which he created, and put these enchanted manacles on my body to ensure that I could never go beyond the confines of this room. Ethindir is gone now, but, alas, I'm still stuck in this enchanted cage."

Christina pointed at the wall. "These gems are beautiful" she said. "What are they called?"

"Reflecting stones," Boriandar replied. "Ethindir used nine thousand, nine hundred ninety-nine of them to build the Room Between the Worlds. They all display your face, even the ones behind you."

"But I don't understand," she said. "They show me frowning, even though I'm not doing that."

"That's because the stones not only show what you look like on the outside, but also what you're feeling on the inside," he said. "You must be a very unhappy person."

This statement made Christina uncomfortable, so she said nothing. Boriandar continued to speak. "I spend most of my time trapped inside these dratted stones and am only allowed to come out under certain circumstances."

"That's awful!"

The wellwight shrugged. "I've grown accustomed to it. And besides, I'm usually in a wonderful enchanted sleep. But enough chatter. It's time to get down to business, Christina."

"You know my name?" she asked in a shocked voice.

"I ought to," Boriandar replied. "You see, I've been watching you for a long time now."

"But how could you see me if you can't leave this room?"

"Look over at the wall."

She did as Boriandar bid her, but the only thing she saw were her reflections. Then the wellwight snapped his fingers, and the stones displayed noisy images of her world; it was like staring at thousands of television sets. She saw people from different places engaging in ordinary activities such as cooking, driving, and playing sports. Boriandar snapped his fingers again and Christina's reflections reappeared. His reflection was strangely absent, even though he hovered close to her.

"But why were you watching *me*?" she asked.

"My job is to find brave and virtuous children from your world and bring them here," Boriandar replied. "I put the Well in that glade because you seemed to be fond of the place. And now that you've arrived, I wish to send you on a quest."

"Really?" She couldn't believe what she was hearing. "What sort of quest?"

"If you choose to go through the portal that lies under your feet, you'll end up in Imar. It's the largest and greatest kingdom in the world of Myredan, which is where I am from. But the current monarch is a tyrant named King James. Under his rule, thousands of innocent Imarians have suffered or been killed. He must be destroyed. The members of the Order of Ethindir will aid you in this task. You'll know them by their medallions, which are round and display an ouroboros in the center."

"What's an ouroboros?" Christina asked.

"It's a serpent that eats its tail and thereby creates an infinite circle," Boriandar replied. "Now please don't interrupt me again, child. You'll face danger and hardship, and you may not survive. But if you triumph, you can take the throne. King James and the other children possessed great virtues when they came to the kingdom but abandoned them over time and became wicked and corrupt. Would you like go on the quest and attempt to succeed where they failed?"

Christina's eyes narrowed, for she felt something amiss here.

"Are you sure you have the right person?" she asked. "I'm not exactly the heroic and virtuous type. And I'm only eleven."

Boriandar smiled. "That's old enough. Many children from your world don't know what they're capable of at first, but I've looked into your soul and seen your virtues. You may not yet realize that you possess them, but you shall in time."

Christina wanted to see the kingdom, but she hesitated.

"I'm not sure I should do this," she said slowly. "If I go on the quest, will I ever be able to go home? Do I have to rule if I succeed?"

"If you come to my world, it will still be possible to return to yours," Boriandar replied. "You'll become the queen the moment King James dies, but you aren't bound to stay even then. I must say though, no child has ever returned. If such a thing had happened, neither of us would be here right now."

"What do you mean?"

"When the old ruler is dead, you'll possess the Elixir of Purity and the Sword of Etossar. As long as you drink the Elixir, you'll be immortal; that is, you'll never age past your thirty-third year. But you can still be killed, of course. And when you drink for the first time, the Sword becomes a magic weapon that enables you to defeat all enemies. But be warned; this great power comes with a price. Your thirst for the Elixir will never cease, your soul will be bound to it for the rest of your life, and the Well shall close to you forever."

"What if I don't drink the Elixir and decide to go home?"

"If you decline the quest, I can open the portal to your world this very moment and send you back. But if you travel through the portal to Imar and wish to return home at a later time, you'll have to destroy the Well. In order to do that, you must bring the Sword and the Elixir to this room. If you return with only the Sword, you'll be trapped in this place until hunger and thirst overtake you. If you return with only the Elixir, you'll have to drink it to go back to the kingdom, or you'll die. Now it's time for you to make your decision, for I don't wish to float up here forever. The search to find you has been an exhausting endeavor, and I want to retire into the reflecting stones and sleep. And know that this offer shall not be repeated. If you don't accept the quest, then I shall find a child who will."

After considering for a minute, Christina decided that the quest was the only way to escape from her present situation. She felt too upset to return home to Mom, who probably didn't want to see her again anyway.

"Alright," she said at last. "I accept."

A smile swept across Boriandar's face, and he grabbed her hand and shook it. Christina shivered, for the wellwight's hand felt like a chilly draft.

"Congratulations!" he said. "You're about to embark upon the quest of a lifetime! Now some advice before you go. When you enter the portal, make sure your head is pointed downward. Good luck to you!"

"Thanks!" she said as the water swirled and formed a whirlpool beneath her feet. Before long, she disappeared into the center of it.

***

As soon as she was underwater, Christina maneuvered her body so that her head faced the bottom of the portal. A mixture of fear and excitement gripped her as she traveled to the kingdom.

The water carried her to the top of the Well on the other side, and she found herself upright. After hoisting herself above the well wall, Christina felt the warmth of a bright morning sun. Looking down, she beheld a vast plain of golden close-cropped grass, which rolled in shimmering waves thanks to a gentle breeze. Dazzled, she couldn't take her eyes from the ethereal sea before her. When she finally looked up, a panorama of mountains, hills, rivers, and forests greeted the new arrival.

Christina jumped to the ground and began walking away from the Well. But she hadn't gone more than ten paces when somebody grabbed her from behind and said in a harsh masculine voice, "Got you, you little troll!"

CHAPTER THREE
ENEMIES AND ALLIES

Christina screamed, kicked, and scratched with all her might, but her captor's grip was firm. When a dagger appeared in front of her face, she thrust her head downward and bit the hand holding the weapon. Her captor cried out in anguish and released his grip, causing her to fall forward. Scrambling to her feet, Christina heard her captor utter another cry but started running without looking back.

"Wait!"

Christina stopped and turned around. A tall man in a suit of gray armor stood next to the Well holding a sword in one hand and a shield in the other. In front of him lay another man whom she guessed was her captor.

"You've come at last!" her rescuer cried. "Of course, I knew you would, but I never imagined that you'd do so on *my* watch! I'm Eorin. What's your name, child?"

Christina was too shocked by her traumatic arrival to respond. After a few moments, she pointed at the man lying on the ground and asked, "Is he dead?"

Eorin nodded.

Greatly upset, Christina stared at the corpse for another minute. The only dead person she had ever seen back in her own world was her great-uncle Andy.

"Who was he?" she asked, looking up to face Eorin.

"Darion, one of the king's loyal soldiers," he replied with a contemptuous snort. "King James left us to guard the Well of Rulers and kill the first child who emerged from it. I, too, am a soldier of the king, but not by choice. I wish to serve *you*, if you'll have me."

"You're not a member of the Order of Ethindir?"

"No, but I will serve you as faithfully as anyone in the Order."

After kneeling before Christina and laying his sword and shield on the ground next to a bulky brown sack that rested near his feet, Eorin grasped her hand and kissed it. His red beard felt scratchy, and she resisted the urge to pull her hand away.

"O child of the World Below, I swear complete allegiance to you and lay my life at your service," he said in a deeply reverent tone.

"The World Below?"

"We Imarians call your world by that name because the rulers reach Imar by traveling up this well," Eorin replied. "However, the children from the World Below call Imar the Kingdom Beneath the Well because they must first go down the two portals in the Well of Rulers in order to reach this land."

She nodded. "You can serve me. My name's Christina, by the way."

"Let me take your bag, Christina," Eorin said, rising to his feet and sliding his sword into the leather scabbard hanging from his waist. She handed over her schoolbag, which he put it in his sack. After slinging the sack over his shoulder and picking up his shield with his free hand, he said, "I must get you away from this place. Come."

Christina stayed put, her mind petrified with uncertainty. Where were the members of the Order? Were they going to pick her up? Was she supposed to wait here by the Well? The idea that something terrible might have happened to them entered her mind, and she tried to suppress it.

"I don't know if I should leave this place," she said cautiously. "Boriandar told me the Order was going to help me. What if they get here and find that I'm gone?"

"I'm not certain," Eorin replied. "But I do know that the king will soon learn of your arrival and send soldiers to the Well. And if you stay here, they might capture you. So it's imperative that we leave immediately."

Seeing the wisdom of this, Christina nodded again. Recalling her recent scare, she decided she didn't want to go through *that* again.

"Where do we go?" she asked.

Eorin looked around and thoughtfully stroked his beard. "The Amber Castle lies over there," he said, pointing east. "That's where the king lives. So I think we should head in the opposite direction, don't you?"

Christina nodded, and the two of them started walking away from the Well.

"I want to thank you for saving my life," she said shyly.

"My pleasure," Eorin replied.

Christina turned her head this way and that and admired the grass, whose sheen cast a dazzling brilliance. The blades resembled tiny spears of metallic gold, and she longed to pick them but refrained from doing so lest they contain some deadly magic.

"This is a beautiful place," she said. "I've never seen golden grass before. It's too pretty to walk on."

"We're on the Plain of Ethindir, the center of our kingdom," Eorin replied. "We Imarians also call this area the Well Plain. After Ethindir created the Well, he surrounded it with this grass."

"What happens if you pluck one of the blades?" she asked.

Eorin shrugged. "It will turn brown."

After she tired of admiring the grass, Christina stared at the emblem on Eorin's shield. It displayed a flask ringed by an ouroboros—which, in turn, was surrounded by a stone circle. In addition, a short sword positioned directly behind the flask lay across the stone and serpentine symbols.

"What's that?" she asked, pointing at the emblem.

"The royal coat of arms," Eorin responded, but before he could say anything further, the two of them heard a swooshing sound overhead. Barely a moment after Eorin raised his shield, an arrow struck the center and remained there. He dropped his sack and pushed Christina to the ground. Standing before her, he drew his sword. Soon she heard a screech and the sound of flapping wings. Peering from behind Eorin's legs, she gasped.

A griffin the size of a pony hovered several feet from the ground in front of them, and two dwarfs sat on his back. Clouds of gold dust rose into the air as he flapped his purple wings. The griffin's tan body, which resembled a lion's, glistened with sweat, and his eagle's head was white and smooth. Staring at Christina through beady black eyes, the creature opened and closed his brown beak.

Hoping that griffins didn't eat children, Christina turned her gaze upon the dwarfs. They were dressed in silver cloaks, and the one sitting in front looked to be the taller of the two; she guessed he was a few inches above four feet. He looked very old, and his wizened face radiated authority and wisdom. His companion was a bit shorter, and his face had the look of youth.

The elder dwarf held a longbow with an arrow pointing at Eorin.

"Get away from the child!" he shouted.

"I'm here to protect her, you fleabag!" Eorin said, his shield still raised, sword at the ready.

"Protecting her is *our* job, human scum!" the older dwarf replied.

Christina stood up and walked out in front of Eorin.

"Take it easy guys," she said to the dwarfs with a trace of annoyance in her voice. "This man just saved my life."

The dwarfs scoffed at this.

"Child, he plans to deliver you alive to King James so he can kill you himself!" the older dwarf said scornfully.

"Dwarf, you're even more dull-witted than you look," Eorin said. "Think, if you—"

Christina raised her hand, and he fell silent.

"We were heading west," she said to the older dwarf. "Eorin here told me the Amber Castle is that way, in the east. Was he telling the truth?"

For a moment, the older dwarf looked dumbfounded. He stared around, furrowed his bushy eyebrows, scratched his ancient yellow beard, and made odd faces as though parts of his mind were at war with one another. At last, he let out an exasperated sigh and said, "Yes, the human spoke the truth."

Christina decided that it was time to change the subject. "What are your names?" she asked the dwarfs. "I'm Christina."

The elder dwarf dismounted from the griffin and bowed. "Gilfoit at your service," he said grandly. "My companion here is called Albrik." He lovingly patted the griffin's head. "And this is Kahlwindor."

"Is that griffin dangerous?" Christina asked as she warily eyed the sharp beak.

Gilfoit shook his head. "Kahlwindor's harmless. Albrik and I are members of the Order of Ethindir, and we're going to take you to the Sanctuary. It lies in the Mironan Mountains, which is north of here. You'll stay there until it's time to build up an army and move against King James."

"Can you guys show me your medallions?" Christina asked.

The dwarfs reached into their cloaks and pulled out silver medallions that glowed brilliantly. Gilfoit looked at Eorin and said grudgingly, "Human, I grant that I may have been mistaken about your intentions, but you no longer need to accompany the child. We'll take it from here."

"I've sworn an oath to protect her to the end, and I mean to keep that oath," Eorin replied.

"He's coming with us," Christina said, ignoring the look of anger on Gilfoit's face. "He wants to serve me, and I owe him that much."

"Child, the human may mean well now," Albrik said, "But he might betray you in the future if doing so enriches him in some way or spares his life."

"I would do no such thing!" Eorin replied indignantly. "I am a man of honor."

Christina looked at Eorin, and doubt suddenly clouded her mind. Was Albrik right? Would Eorin betray her if it was in his interest to do so? Maybe. Back in her own world, Sylvia and her father had abandoned her over matters less important than the possibility of death. Gilfoit and Albrik could be trusted because they were members of the Order, but what about a soldier of the king?

After considering the matter, she said, "Eorin stays with me. He willingly endangered his own life by killing his companion and saving mine, so I say he's trustworthy." When Gilfoit and Albrik started to protest, she held up a hand and added, "And that's final."

"Very well," Gilfoit replied with a sigh. "Now we must hasten to the Sanctuary. Kahlwindor can fly swiftly, but it'll take several days for us to reach the mountains." He smirked at Eorin. "Four is too heavy for a griffin of this size, so I suppose you'll have to find another means of travel."

"Of course!" Eorin replied sarcastically. "Any excuse to keep me from coming along!"

"It's true I'd rather you stayed behind," Gilfoit admitted, "But I wasn't lying when I said that Kahlwindor can't carry so heavy a load."

"If Kahlwindor can't take all of us, then Eorin and I will walk to the Sanctuary, and you two can fly," Christina said.

"It's your decision," Gilfoit replied with a shrug. "But I shall accompany you in case this human turns out to be a scoundrel."

Eorin scowled but made no reply. Gilfoit looked up at Albrik and said, "Fly to Lord Evermore and tell him the child has arrived, and that we're on our way to the Sanctuary."

Happy to be given such an important task, Albrik beamed and nodded excitedly. He gave a command, and Kahlwindor turned around and flew away. As she watched those beautiful wings flap in the air, Christina felt a twinge of regret for not agreeing to fly to the mountains.

Gilfoit reached into a brown pouch slung across his chest and pulled out a small black cloak.

"Put this on," he said, handing it to Christina. When she did, he nodded. "Good. Now you look like a human child from our world. We mustn't let anyone know who you really are until the time is right. Now let's leave this place at once."

CHAPTER FOUR
THE HORSELESS KNIGHT

After walking north a few miles, the trio reached the end of the plain and traveled along a stone road that snaked its way through a green land of fields and hillocks. Sweat poured down Christina's face, but she was thankful the weather was sunny and clear; after all, walking in a rainstorm would be *much* worse.

As the travelers rounded a steep hillock, she saw an armored man sitting on top of a smooth square boulder. He was sobbing, his face buried in his arms. Christina walked up to him and asked, "Are you alright?"

The man raised his head and pushed up the visor on his helmet. "No, I'm not, child," he sniffed. "My life is doomed."

"What's wrong? What's your name? Mine's Christina, and this is Gilfoit and Eorin," she said, gesturing toward her two companions.

The man nodded his head by way of greeting. "Sir Owenday at your service," he said in a pitiful voice.

"You're a knight?" Eorin asked.

Sir Owenday nodded, tears trickling down his black beard.

"If you're a knight, then where's your horse?" Gilfoit asked.

"The answer lies in a tale of woe," the knight said. "I can tell it to you, if you like."

"I'd love to hear it!" Christina said, sitting on the ground next to the knight's sword and shield.

"We shouldn't be wasting any time with stories," Gilfoit said sternly.

"But a short break might do us some good," Eorin remarked.

Gilfoit sighed and looked at the horseless knight. "Very well. But make it brief. We have a long journey ahead of us."

After Gilfoit and Eorin sat on the ground next to Christina, Sir Owenday began his story.

"I earned my knighthood at a very young age, and I was one of the best knights in the kingdom. And I had a magnificent purebred horse named Darigoble. But I was cruel and vain. I liked to frequent taverns and start fights, especially with those weaker than myself. I treated women badly and even thrashed children who crossed my path. One night, I left a tavern very drunk and rode my horse all over the countryside. As I sped down a dirt path, shouting like a fool, I nearly ran over a young woman. She must have been a witch because she shot a curse, and it hit me in the back of the head. That sobered me up straightaway. I had a terrible headache, and I knew it couldn't have come as a result of the spirits I'd drank because that sort of thing doesn't usually happen to me until the next morning. I looked around, but the witch was nowhere to be seen. When I mounted Darigoble, he screamed and threw me to the ground. I tried to mount him again, but he ran off. The next morning, I acquired a different horse, but the same thing happened. The witch put a curse on me so I could never ride a horse again. I saw other witches, but they told me that the only person who could take the curse off was the one who put it on. So I left my estate and searched the kingdom for the witch who cursed me, but I never found her."

"How unfortunate," Eorin said sympathetically.

Sir Owenday hung his head. "No matter where I go, I'm treated with ridicule by the other knights. They laugh at me and exclude me from their tournaments. But I can't say I blame them, for I used to treat my peers as badly as I treated everyone else. Now I'm embarrassed to even show my face."

"But you're not necessarily grounded, are you?" Gilfoit asked. "Couldn't you ride another animal?"

"I could but have no desire to," Sir Owenday sighed. "There is no greater bond than the one between a knight and his horse. My life was never complete without Darigoble, and now he's gone."

"I know what you mean," Christina said. "I love horses. I don't own one, but I've always wanted to."

Sir Owenday nodded. "Everything is hopeless. Never again will I be a true knight. But I deserve this fate."

"I'm sure you have other things going for you," Christina said in an attempt to lift his spirits. "I'll bet you're great with a sword."

"True. I'm a skilled warrior."

"There you have it," Eorin said. "I'm sure an army somewhere would love to recruit you."

"The only army around here is the one belonging to King James," Sir Owenday replied. "And I would *never* enter the service of that tyrant."

"You could come with us, Sir Owenday," Christina said, ignoring the look of consternation on Gilfoit's face. "We're traveling to the Mironan Mountains, and we could use another warrior. Maybe the trip will help you forget your troubles."

"I'd like that, child," Sir Owenday sniffed, looking at her with interest. "Perhaps I could protect you?"

"Sure," Christina said, smiling. "You'll be my personal bodyguard."

Sir Owenday's gloom disappeared as he knelt before her, grabbed her hand, and planted a soft kiss. "I lay my sword and life at your service, Christina," he said.

"I think we had best be going," Gilfoit said with exasperation.

CHAPTER FIVE
EELWEED

After an hour's walk, the company reached a stone bridge spanning a wide river. Ornate parapets ran across the sides of the bridge, and Christina heard the sound of rushing water.

"This is the Sicudor River, the longest in the kingdom and home of the water gnomes," Gilfoit said.

Christina looked down into the green water in the hope of spotting one of the creatures, but all she saw was a school of red fish swimming upstream. The travelers crossed the bridge, and the road on the other side continued across a long stretch of black sand. Up ahead, Christina saw tiny sparkling trees and hills. Pointing at them, she asked, "What's that?"

"The glass country of Ifartheon," Gilfoit replied. "That's where the miniatures live."

"Miniatures? You mean little humans?"

"Yes."

"How small are they? What are they like?"

"The adults don't usually grow above two inches," Eorin replied. "They keep to themselves, and the other humans and creatures ignore them. We'll pass through the glass country on our way to the mountains."

"But if we're so much bigger than the miniatures, won't we cause a lot of damage to their land?" Christina asked.

"Don't worry, child," Gilfoit said. "The Ifarthians keep a road for us giant folk. It's just up ahead."

Christina hoped to see a miniature during the journey through Ifartheon. Any person that made a dwarf such as Gilfoit look like a giant caught her interest.

Suddenly, someone behind them shouted, "I beg your pardon, Imarians!"

The travelers turned around and saw a water gnome running up to them. When he was a few paces away, he stopped. The creature was a foot shorter than Gilfoit, and he wore a coat made of clam shells. A short curved sword hung from his seaweed belt, and a harpoon was strapped to his back.

"What do you want?" Eorin asked impatiently, his hand on the hilt of his own sword.

"Please, sir," the stranger replied. "I mean you no harm. Eelweed's my name. May I ask where you folks are traveling today?"

"To the Mironan Mountains," Christina said. She couldn't take her eyes off this green stranger. He fascinated her with his rubbery webbed feet, hair resembling dark seaweed, and gills behind his pointy ears.

"The mountains!" Eelweed cried. "I've always wanted to see them! May I come with you?"

"No," Gilfoit said shortly. "This company is too large as it is. You'll only slow us down."

"Why do you want to come to the mountains with us?" Christina asked.

"I'm running away," Eelweed said.

This piqued her interest. "How come?"

"I'm servant to a water gnome baron who runs a dragon turtle farm, but I wish to go on adventures and see strange places," he replied. "Would you folks grant me the privilege of accompanying you? I wouldn't be a burden, I promise you. I can catch fish, and when it comes to danger, I'm quite deadly with this harpoon and sword. Please say you'll let me come!"

"Sorry, water gnome, but you can't," Gilfoit said. "Now we must be moving along. You'll have to wait for someone else to take you to the mountains." He gave Christina a stern look, and she decided not to oppose him this time.

"I'm sorry, Eelweed," she said. "But Gil is right. I'm sure you'll find another traveling companion soon."

And with that, the company left the dejected water gnome standing alone on the road.

CHAPTER SIX
THE MINIATURE KNIGHT

Entering Ifartheon, the company walked along a road made of smooth, clear glass stones cobbled together and crisscrossed by cracks forming beautiful spider web patterns. On one side of the road, a shoulder-high forest stood, while on the other side, hills rolled across the landscape. Christina could see cottages and tiny people off in the distance. Everything and everyone appeared to be made of glass that glimmered in the sunlight. Although this miniature land resembled the larger one with its brown trees and green fields, the Ifarthians themselves were all different colors.

"How big is Ifartheon?" she asked, her eyes devouring the wonders of this spectacular land.

"Not very large to us giant folk," Sir Owenday replied. "This road runs across the entire glass country and it's only four miles. But to the miniatures, this land is huge."

Christina pointed and said, "There's a purple glass knight sitting on a red horse up ahead of us. Gil, I thought you said only giant folks use this road."

"They do," he replied. "Keep walking. That Ifarthian will move out of our way."

But when the travelers came within a few inches of the knight, he didn't move. Instead, he waved his sword and cried out, "You may not travel any farther, strangers!"

The knight's words caused the company to stop. Gilfoit glared down at him and growled, "Hasten out of our way, or I shall ground you and your steed to powder."

"I'd like to see you try, dwarf!" the tiny interloper replied. "I'm not afraid of you or any other giant folk. Why, I could smite all of you!"

"Now there, let's not be hasty," Sir Owenday said. "Sir Knight, why do you block our path? We have done you no harm."

The glass knight pointed his sword at Gilfoit. "That fiend insulted me!" he said. "He didn't address me by my proper title!"

"Why did you block our way in the first place?" Christina demanded.

"Do not question my actions, human child," he replied, "Or I shall forget my chivalric oath and smite you."

"Stop it!" Eorin cried. "That's no way to talk to your future queen!"

The glass knight gasped, and so did Gilfoit, who looked at Eorin with fury.

"Why don't you just tell the whole kingdom who she is?" the dwarf said sarcastically.

Eorin gave no reply to this, but his face was a deep scarlet.

Sir Owenday slapped his shield. "I thought there was something different about you!" he said, looking at Christina with a smile on his face.

The glass knight stared up at her with disbelief. "You're a child from the World Below?"

When she nodded, he leapt from his horse and went on one knee before her. "Please accept my apologies, Your Majesty," he said. "I'm called Sir Kranwick, and I give you my allegiance."

"I'm not the queen yet, so you don't have to address me like one," she said. "Call me 'Christina'."

Sir Kranwick mounted his horse. "Thank you, Your Majesty. But I think it's fitting to call you by that title, since it won't be long before that scoundrel King James is dead."

"Well, nice to meet you," Christina said. "We'd better move along now. We need to get to the Mironan Mountains."

"It would give me great pleasure if Her Majesty would allow me to accompany her," said the glass knight.

"I'm not sure that's a good idea," Christina replied doubtfully. "This company has enough members in it, and you might not be able to keep up with the rest of us."

"That shan't be a problem," Sir Kranwick said, patting his horse's mane. "Crossander here is very fast and strong. And the road ahead may hold unforeseen dangers. The more Imarians you have traveling with you, the safer you'll be."

"Alright," she replied in a cheerful voice. "Let's go."

Gilfoit shook his head and muttered something inaudible under his breath.

***

As the company continued its journey, Christina asked Sir Kranwick why he tried to stop them.

"I wanted to start a duel," he said. "I spend most of my time on this road attempting to provoke human and creature travelers into fighting me. But it never works. They just laugh at me and continue on their way."

"How is it you can be made of glass and still move and talk?" she asked.

"I don't quite understand, Your Majesty," he replied, a confused look on his face. "What does being made of glass have to do with these abilities or lack thereof?"

"In my world, miniatures aren't alive."

"How very strange," Sir Owenday remarked.

"How many miniatures live in Ifartheon?" Christina asked.

"There are over three million of us," Sir Kranwick said proudly.

She whistled in amazement. "What kinds of things do miniatures like to do?"

"We do the same things you giant folk do," Sir Kranwick said matter-of-factly. "Ifarthians farm, hunt, and engage in commerce. But our favorite pastime is preparing for war. Ifartheon possesses the largest army in the kingdom; numerically speaking, that is. In fact, I'm the commander of the army, and the best warrior in the land. Our greatest desire is to go to war and fight with the giant folk, and we train constantly for battle. However, our fellow Imarians never take us seriously. The only battles waged in this kingdom are those of rebellion and succession, but nobody requests our services because of our small stature. Alas, I fear I shall never get into Aressindor."

"Aressindor?" Christina asked.

"Every warrior in our world who fights courageously in battle goes there when they die," Eorin told her. "Those who enter the gates of Aressindor get to feast in the Great Hall."

"When the time comes to fight King James, you and your people can help us," Christina said to Sir Kranwick.

The glass knight's eyes narrowed. "I beg your pardon, Your Majesty, but are you pulling my chainmail?"

She smiled. "Of course not. I don't consider you of no use. After all, you challenged us, and we're a lot bigger. You must be very brave."

"Thank you, Your Majesty!" Sir Kranwick said. "This day has turned out be a great one for me. It's nice to have some excitement for once. Life here in Ifartheon is rather dull."

"Where is your home?" Sir Owenday asked.

"I live in the estate of Gormaille," Sir Kranwick replied. "It lies about ten miniature leagues to the west of this road."

He suddenly raised his hand and cried, "Halt!"

Everyone stopped and waited patiently while a glass shepherd and his sheep emerged from the forest and crossed the road to reach the hills on the other side. To Christina, the tiny animals' bleating sounded like twinkling bells.

After the company walked another mile, the glass road ended, and a coarse path of dirt and stone led into a forest. Two trees on either side of the path bent at angles to form a narrow arch. The other trees stood so close together that Christina couldn't see behind them.

"This is Ferncandell Forest, the largest in Imar," Gilfoit said to her.

"Is it safe?" she asked warily. The place looked eerie in the early twilight.

Gilfoit shrugged. "It's as safe as any other place in the kingdom. Hopefully, this path will lead us straight through the forest. If it does, we can reach the Grassland of Morlinduhl without difficulty as long as we're not bothered by any unwelcome parties. The Mironan Mountains are on the other side of the grassland."

CHAPTER SEVEN
GILFOIT'S TALE

The company entered Ferncandell Forest single file, with Gilfoit in the lead. Christina walked behind him, Eorin behind her, and Sir Owenday brought up the rear while Sir Kranwick and Crossander rested on his shoulder. When she saw the forest, Christina gasped.

There were trees of all different shapes and sizes. Many of them—such as oaks, firs, pines, and redwoods—were familiar to her, but others had an exotic look. Some trees had square trunks and resembled giant boxes with branches sticking out. Christina especially liked the donut-shaped trees whose branches extended into the hole in the middle and crisscrossed one another. Trees standing hundreds of feet tall blotted out part of the sky with their thick limbs and multi-colored leaves while saplings vied for space with shrubs and strange-looking plants in the dense undergrowth. The path was clear, but on either side, glittering emerald moss and grass blanketed the ground.

"This place is beautiful!" Christina said, admiring a butterfly with purple and blue wings that glowed. "Do people live here?"

"Humans don't usually live in Ferncandell Forest, but tree gnomes and waulds do," Gilfoit replied.

"What are waulds?" Christina asked.

"Giant men who wear black hooded cloaks and carry wooden pikes," Eorin replied. "They're the guardians of the forest."

"Will we get to see them?" Christina asked excitedly.

"Not anytime soon," Gilfoit replied. "Most of the creatures in Ferncandell dwell in the center. Folks say a shape-shifter named Lord Bodwar lives there as well. Legend has it he can change from a man to a bear at will. He has dominion over many of the creatures and beasts in the forest, but only the ruler of Imar has dominion over him."

***

An hour passed before the travelers set up camp in a large tree grove located about forty feet from the path. Gilfoit made a fire while Eorin hunted for meat. The soldier soon returned with the carcass of a red boar. While Sir Kranwick and his horse ate their miniature glass food, the other travelers cooked the boar on straight branches. Christina wolfed down her meat, for she was very hungry, and she opened her schoolbag and passed around the graham crackers that she had packed for her journey. The Imarians enjoyed them greatly and thanked her.

During the meal, Christina heard a soft tittering behind her. Turning her head, she saw several tiny people sitting on a branch of a donut-shaped tree. They were as big as Sir Kranwick and wore brown and green outfits. Staring at Christina and her companions with looks of merriment on their pink faces, the people giggled uncontrollably and chattered with each other in a language that sounded like playful gibberish.

"What are they?" Christina asked.

"Wood pixies," Gilfoit replied. "Ferncandell Forest is full of them."

"Are they dangerous?"

"No," Sir Owenday said. "But they like to play pranks on giant folk. Once, when I was traveling through here, a group of pixies snuck up on me as I slept and cut part of my beard off."

"Can they speak our language?" she asked.

Eorin shook his head. "The pixies have their own tongue that only they can understand."

When supper was over, Gilfoit, Sir Owenday, and Eorin took out their pipes and sent spiral smoke rings into the air. When Eorin offered Christina his pipe, she shook her head and informed him that smoking gives people cancer. The soldier looked confused for a moment, then shrugged his shoulders and kept puffing away.

Gilfoit stared at the girl as he smoked his own carcinogenic pipe. "I expect you have many questions for me, child," he said.

"Oh lots of questions!" Christina replied. "Why did Ethindir create the Well, the Elixir of Purity, and the Sword of Etossar? And why does Boriandar bring children from my world to rule this place?"

Gilfoit set his pipe on the ground. "Imar was once many kingdoms," he said. "In the easternmost human realm, there lived a young ruler named Haroldine. Her father died when she was twenty years of age, and on the day after Haroldine was crowned queen, she took her army and marched on the other human realms and conquered them with astonishing speed. Under her command, this force defeated armies that were many times greater. Then, she directed her attention toward the creature realms and conquered those, too. In less than a year, she ruled over the largest kingdom in Myredan, and because of this, she became known far and wide as Haroldine the Great. She renamed her newly-expanded kingdom 'Imar' after her father, and her original kingdom and place of residence became known as the Eminent Dominion. Haroldine lived to be a hundred and twenty years old, and Imar enjoyed a century of peace under her reign."

"Humans can live that long in this world?" Christina interrupted.

Gilfoit nodded. "It is unusual for humans, but it does happen sometimes, and many creatures live even longer. Now, as I was saying, Haroldine was a great queen, and a wise one, too. But her son, Adorek, was a corrupt tyrant. Revolts soon broke out and engulfed the entire kingdom. For a while, the dissolution of Imar appeared inevitable."

"Why didn't it happen?" Christina asked.

"Because Ethindir prevented it," Gilfoit replied. "He was a sorcerer of immense power. At the time of the revolts, he lived under Etossar, the highest peak in the Mironan range. His compassion for Imar compelled him to leave his home, destroy the royal family, and defeat their army. Unity and harmony returned to the land. Imarians begged Ethindir to be their king, but he had no desire to wield power over others. However, he agreed to serve as Steward of the Kingdom until he found a suitable human or creature to become the new ruler. To this end, he made the

Elixir of Purity and the Sword of Etossar, which he planned to give to a young Imarian who possessed the virtues of wisdom, courage, ambition, kindness, and truthfulness. Such a ruler, he believed, would provide the kingdom with an eternity of peace and greatness."

Gilfoit paused to send smoke spirals into the air. They rose several feet before flitting away into the firelight.

"What happened?" Christina asked eagerly. "Wasn't Ethindir able to get the ruler he wanted?"

"Ethindir found many humans and creatures who appeared to be worthy choices, but all of them went astray," Gilfoit replied. "And because none of Haroldine's successors managed to reign in a pure manner for longer than the hundred years of her rule, this strange phenomenon became known throughout the land as Haroldine's Curse. Ethindir concluded that there must be some dark force in the kingdom that corrupted the souls of even its most virtuous inhabitants, so he decided to look elsewhere for a ruler. After building the Well, he traveled through the portal and ended up in your world. He journeyed far and wide until he found a promising orphan boy named Primoran. The latter accepted Ethindir's offer to take the throne, and they traveled to Imar. The sorcerer returned to his mountain, and King Primoran turned out to be the greatest ruler since Haroldine. When his peaceful reign surpassed the one-hundred-year mark, Haroldine's Curse was finally broken. Everyone believed that Ethindir had finally found a being with an incorruptible soul. However, the sorcerer wasn't certain of this and decided to keep the Well in place."

"What happened then?" Christina asked.

"His suspicions were confirmed when Primoran turned into a cruel tyrant after three hundred years on the throne. So Ethindir destroyed him and ended up making many trips to the World Below in his effort to find a boy or girl who could rule with absolute power and immortality while forever retaining the virtues that made a great monarch."

Suddenly, the company heard the sound of twigs snapping nearby.

"What was that?" Christina said, looking around in alarm.

"I'd better check," Eorin replied, rising to his feet, sword in hand. After making a quick but thorough search of the area, he returned to the fire and sat down. "I didn't see anything."

"Doubtless, some of those dratted pixies made a little noise to frighten us," Sir Kranwick added. "Unfortunately for them, I don't frighten easily."

Christina calmed down and turned to Gilfoit, who continued his tale.

"But all of the children Ethindir brought to the kingdom came to the same terrible end as their predecessors. He concluded that absolute power corrupts all humans and creatures, regardless of where they hail from. But the rulers from your world were special. As I've said, no monarch from our world ruled for more than a hundred years before going astray, but the children from the World Below could rule for several hundred years before reaching that point. Ethindir never discovered why this was so. After resuming the position of Steward of the Kingdom, he used his power to enhance the process of monarchal replacement so that it would continue after his death. He even gave it a name: The Cycle of Royal Succession."

Gilfoit paused to take a few more puffs. His story was the most exciting Christina had ever heard—and all the more so because she knew that she was a part of it. Eorin, Sir Owenday, and Sir Kranwick also listened to the tale with interest. Christina tried to imagine ruling a kingdom for hundreds of years, but the idea was too fantastic for a girl who felt that a normal school week lasted forever.

Gilfoit continued speaking. "Ethindir built the Room Between the Worlds and brought Boriandar there to serve as Keeper of the Well because wellwights are among the few beings in our world that don't require magic to possess immortality. And because Ethindir believed the children of the World Below should have a choice about whether or not to rule the kingdom after destroying their predecessors, he made it possible for them to return. Yet, of the many children who came to Imar, none chose to leave."

"Why?" Christina asked.

"Like humans and creatures everywhere, they desire power, be it the power to do good or ill," Gilfoit replied. "And once they have power and immortality in their grasp, they're unable to let them go."

Christina pondered this for a moment. "If everyone wants power and immortality, wouldn't a lot of Imarians try to steal the Elixir and Sword and use their magic?" she asked.

"Ethindir altered the Elixir so that it can't be drunk by any human or creature from our world," Gilfoit replied. "If an Imarian swallowed so much as a drop, he would suffer an agonizing death."

"Would something bad happen to me if I drank the Elixir before King James died?" Christina asked.

"No," Gilfoit said. "If you tried to drink it this very moment, the Elixir would simply run down the front of your body. The same thing would happen if someone tried to force it down your throat after the old ruler died. When you drink for the first time, you must do so of your own accord. After that, you can summon the flask into your hand merely by wishing for it. But drinking from it makes you forget about your life in the World Below, and you can never have children of your own who might wish to inherit the throne. And when rulers depart from their virtues and embark upon the path of wickedness, the Elixir darkens, and it's impossible to return to the way of goodness because of the corrupting influence of absolute power. Ethindir also changed the Sword so that its magic could only be wielded by the rulers. Once you drink the Elixir for the first time, the blade glows, and you can summon the sword from anywhere. But when the Elixir darkens, the blade stops glowing and loses its power. Boriandar then awakes from his slumber and searches for a new ruler."

Thinking about the Elixir's power to rub out memories of the World Below gave Christina a creepy feeling in the pit of her stomach. The idea of forgetting about Sylvia and the rest of her schoolmates appealed to her, but she didn't want to forget Dad, or even Mom. And the thought of never being able to have children of her own disturbed her.

"What about the Order?" she asked, changing the subject. "Was it founded after Ethindir's death?"

"No, Ethindir founded it shortly before he died," Gilfoit replied, putting his pipe away. "Our emblem is the ouroboros, which symbolizes the Cycle. If you've seen Eorin's shield, you must have noticed that the ouroboros is on the royal coat of arms, which also displays the Sword of Etossar, the golden flask containing the Elixir, and the Well itself."

"How many members are in the Order?" Christina asked. "Who is your leader? What kinds of creatures are involved?"

"The Order consists of a hundred humans and dwarfs. Lord Evermore is our leader, and as Head of the Order, he also assumes the role of Steward of the Kingdom if a monarch dies before a successor arrives or is otherwise unable to rule. He is not only a great leader and warrior but also a seer whose predictions have all come to pass."

"I've heard of this Lord Evermore," Sir Owenday said breathlessly. "Folks say he is a great and wise man."

Gilfoit nodded.

"Did Ethindir make your medallions?" Eorin asked.

"Yes," Gilfoit replied. "They contain the only magical powers he granted us. The medallions glow when a child from the World Below is near. They turn to gold once an old ruler is dead and revert to silver when the Elixir darkens."

"Impressive," Sir Kranwick remarked.

"And these medallions can do much more," Gilfoit said proudly. "They make us immortal so long as the Well exists. That is, we can't die of natural causes, for we've never aged since putting them on. But we *can* be killed. And the medallions provide sustenance in times of need. We can live without food and water for months, even years, though we'll still feel hunger and thirst. Thanks to our medallions, we've stayed alive for over eight thousand years."

Christina gasped. *"You're over eight thousand years old?"*

Gilfoit nodded and grinned.

"But what about Albrik?" she asked. "It's hard to believe he could be *that* old."

"Albrik was only nineteen when he joined the Order," Gilfoit replied with a grimace. "As a result, he's managed to appear young these last eight millennia. Unfortunately for me, I was already very old when I received my medallion."

"What would happen if someone stole your medallion?" Sir Kranwick asked.

"No one can take my medallion off. And its power disappears the moment I die."

"Why didn't Ethindir make a medallion for himself?" Christina asked.

"He didn't desire immortality," Gilfoit replied. "But he drank the Elixir to prolong his life while he searched for suitable children to rule the kingdom."

"He sounds amazing," she said.

Gilfoit nodded. "He was. The Cycle has granted us many long ages of peace in exchange for short periods of oppression and turmoil. And it has allowed Imar to remain the largest and greatest kingdom in Myredan while all others have disappeared in the desert of time and memory."

As Christina mulled over Gilfoit's words, she felt gloomy. Eorin asked, "What's wrong, child?"

"If I succeed in the quest and take the throne, I'll become like the other rulers and be killed myself," she replied. "I should have known there was a catch."

"Ah, but I haven't told you the final part of the tale," Gilfoit replied. "Shortly after Ethindir's passing, Lord Evermore made a prophecy based on a dream he had."

After clearing his throat, the dwarf recited:

> "When the One ascends to power,
>
> The Elixir shall never sour.
>
> So comes the Cycle's final hour."

"What does that mean?" Christina asked.

"According to this prophecy," Gilfoit replied, "When this extraordinary ruler ascended to the throne, the Elixir's color would never darken, the ruler's reign would never be marked by evil, and the Cycle would be broken forever. And we Imarians would no longer have to rely upon the Well to preserve our kingdom. We call it the Prophecy of the Eternal Ruler."

Christina's gloom disappeared, and she became interested. "Did Lord Evermore say what this ruler would look like or when he—or she—would come?"

"No," Gilfoit replied. "But he said all Imarians will know that the Eternal Ruler sits on the throne when the Elixir remains white after a thousand years of rule. In addition, I believe this ruler will prove to be unlike the others in some special way. Dozens of children have come from the World Below, and it's only a matter of time before the Eternal Ruler arrives. And when he or she does, the kingdom shall enjoy an eternity of peace and greatness. And now we must rest, for we have a long journey ahead of us."

After he handed Christina a wool blanket, she lay on the grass and used her schoolbag as a pillow. Gilfoit, Sir Owenday, and Sir Kranwick made their beds and soon fell asleep while Eorin stood watch. But Christina stayed awake. Sleep was out of the question, for Gilfoit had given her much to consider.

Her mind was a battle zone in which different thoughts and emotions grappled with one another for dominance. Although she was excited about her quest—despite her close call at the Well—she wasn't entirely certain that she wanted to remain in Imar when it was over, and this realization surprised her. She fantasized about becoming the Eternal Ruler, but at the same time, the idea of being forever lost to her own world and never having children bothered her greatly. Christina had often dreamed of living in a magical kingdom, but for the first time in her life, she realized that imagining things and seeing them become reality were two different things.

CHAPTER EIGHT
DEAD END

The days dragged on as the company trudged through Ferncandell Forest. As they moved deeper into the enchanted woodland, the trees huddled closer together, and thin shafts of golden sunlight filtered through the dense, high canopy. At Gilfoit's insistence, they walked all morning, afternoon, and part of the evening and took only a few breaks during the day. The travelers said little to one another, and Christina felt exhausted all of the time. To make matters worse, the warm weather and thick cloak made her sweat profusely.

During the early part of her journey through Ferncandell Forest, she had amused herself by gazing at its strange wonders: the perytons who possessed the head and body of a deer and the wings of a bird; the translucent stags that blended with the surrounding environment like chameleons; the emerald sylvans who danced during the late hours. But as time wore on, she felt disappointed at not seeing a tree gnome or a wauld, and tedium set in. This wasn't the way things were supposed to be. The quests she read about were filled with nonstop excitement, not endless hours of monotony. Christina wanted to complain but deemed this behavior unfit for a queen.

On the company's seventh day in the forest, the trees began to thin out again and sunlight flooded the path.

"Gil, how much longer do we have to go in this place?" Christina asked.

"We're approaching the northern boundary of Ferncandell Forest," he replied. "Perhaps we'll reach the grassland after another—"

Swoosh!

Something flew far above the trees.

"That sounds like a griffin," Eorin said. "And it's coming our way. We'd best hide in case the rider turns out to be an enemy."

"Let them come!" Sir Kranwick cried, waving his tiny sword. "If it's an enemy, I'll take him myself!"

"Do as I say, you little fool!" Eorin hissed, glaring down at the miniature knight.

For once, Sir Kranwick didn't argue. He followed the others into a nearby hedge, where they all waited. Gilfoit slowly pulled an arrow from his quiver and nocked it. Eorin and Sir Owenday unscabbarded their swords. Since Christina had nothing on hand to fight with, she picked up some sharp stones that lay nearby. The swooshing sound grew louder, and two familiar figures landed on the path before them.

"Albrik! Kahlwindor!" Gilfoit cried as he and the others emerged from their hiding place.

The ancient but youthful-looking dwarf dismounted from the griffin and bowed. After Gilfoit introduced Albrik to Sir Owenday and Sir Kranwick, he asked, "Any news of the king?"

"Yes," Albrik replied. "King James learned of Christina's arrival shortly after she came out of the Well. He's sent out soldiers and the best bounty seekers in the kingdom to find her. Have you not encountered them already?"

Gilfoit shook his head. "We haven't seen anyone." Turning to Christina, he said, "You must ride with Albrik the rest of the way. You can avoid the king's men and reach the Sanctuary much sooner. I'll meet you there."

"It's too late for that," Albrik replied. "King James has filled the skies between the mountains and the Well Plain with soldiers on perytons and griffins. I was stopped and questioned only a few hours ago."

"Very well," Gilfoit said. "Tell Lord Evermore that we're almost out of the forest and should reach the mountains in a few days."

Albrik nodded. "Good luck!"

He mounted Kahlwindor and they rose into the air and disappeared through the trees. The company traveled the rest of the day and made a fire shortly before sunset. After dinner, Sir Owenday stood watch while the others slept.

***

When Christina was awakened by a hand grabbing her shoulder, she opened her eyes, expecting to see one of her companions. Instead, an ugly, warty face stared into hers, and she screamed. The face belonged to a huge man wearing a brown surcoat. Through her peripheral vision, she spotted Gilfoit, Eorin, and Sir Owenday surrounded by men in armor. Their wrists were tied behind their backs. Sir Kranwick was nowhere to be seen. She tried to get away, but the man

54

held her in a viselike grip. With his free hand, he shoved a glowing blue phial in front of her face.

"Well, Gorgrin," someone behind her said. "Is it the child?"

Gorgrin nodded and smiled, displaying a row of crooked yellow teeth. "It's her," he said, turning to a short, pudgy man standing next to him. "Larindar, bind her wrists."

Larindar pulled Christina to her feet, tied her wrists tightly behind her back, and shoved her next to her companions. It was dark, but she could see her captors because most of them carried torches. There were several dozen men in armor, some in cloaks, and a handful of dwarfs. One of the men held up her schoolbag and stared at it curiously.

Gorgrin faced his prisoners, the smile still on his face. "Let's take them to His Majesty and collect our reward!" he said to his companions, who replied with cheers.

As the captors led Christina and her friends deeper into the forest, she turned her head toward Gilfoit and whispered out of the corner of her mouth, "Where's Sir Kranwick?"

"I haven't seen him since we lay down to sleep," he replied softly. "Doubtless, the little braggart fled at the first sign of trouble."

"How did these bounty seekers find us?"

"The Elixir causes the flask or anything else containing it to glow when a child from the World Below is near," Gilfoit replied. "Wicked rulers will pour it into small phials and distribute them to their soldiers and bounty seekers to help them track down their successors."

"Silence!" one of their captors shouted, cuffing Gilfoit on the ear. The pair said no more.

After several more hours of walking, the captors led their charges into a vast glade dotted with tents and illuminated by rows of torches. Christina saw hundreds of human soldiers and creatures. At the far end of the glade sat an enormous golden chair flanked by two hideous-looking ogres wearing silver armor and carrying maces. A diamond-shaped table stood next to the chair, and a golden flask filled with black liquid was perched on top of it. A tall man wearing a gold crown and a purple robe with gold cuffs lounged in the chair.

It was King James.

CHAPTER NINE
THE KING OF IMAR

When the prisoners were hauled in front of the monarch, Gorgrin grabbed a handful of Christina's hair and shook violently, causing her to shriek in pain. He held the phial up to her face again and stared at the king.

"Your Majesty, we've caught the usurper, along with a member of the Order, the soldier who betrayed you, and this horseless knight," he said before releasing her hair with a jerk of his hand.

Upon rising, King James screwed up his face, and the flask flew into his outstretched hand. The moment he uncorked the stopper, a geyser of black elixir shot into the air like oil spewing from the ground. As the king took a long drink of the Elixir, some of the liquid poured down the front of his robe and disappeared. It occurred to Christina that if King James's hazel eyes weren't filled with malevolence, and if his mouth weren't curled into a sneer, he would have looked rather handsome, with his youthful freckled face and curly brown hair.

"What's your name, girl?" he asked harshly, sealing the flask.

"Christina," she replied.

"Christina, I know you've come to take my throne, but you shan't have it!" King James said, reaching into his robe and pulling out a sword with a short, gleaming silver blade and a diamond-encrusted hilt.

"Magnificent, isn't it?" King James said. "This is the Sword of Etossar. I acquired it over three hundred years ago after I destroyed my predecessor. I alone am the rightful ruler of the Kingdom Beneath the Well! Do you think I'm going to let a usurper like yourself take what is mine?" He leaned closer and looked straight into her eyes. "I'm going to kill you, Christina. I'm going to cut off your head and the head of any other children who come up the Well of Rulers."

The king looked at Gilfoit and said, "I remember you. You once helped me take the throne, and now you've turned against me. You and the Order took me to the Sanctuary in the mountains, but that was a long time ago. I no longer remember where it is, and my soldiers can't find it. Tell me the location, and I'll spare your life."

"No," Gilfoit replied curtly.

The king's eyes flashed with anger. "No, *what?*"

"I beg your pardon?" Gilfoit said, feigning ignorance.

"No, *Your Majesty*," the king snarled.

Gilfoit grinned. "Sorry, but I'm not the new ruler," he said, jerking his head in Christina's direction. "She is."

Gorgrin punched Gilfoit's right cheek and caused him to fall against Eorin. One of the captors grabbed the dwarf and held him steady.

"I shall get the information from you one way or another," the king said before turning to Sir Owenday. "Who are you and how did you come to be in the usurper's company? Speak up!"

"Sir Owenday. I'm her bodyguard."

"For your treason, you shall share the girl's fate."

"I'm not afraid to die," the knight said defiantly.

Ignoring this last reply, the king looked at Eorin and said, "I recognize you. You're one of the soldiers I sent to guard the Well. My men found your dead companion lying next to it. They told me he was stabbed in the back of the neck. Did you do that?"

"Yes."

King James's eyes flickered. "You swore an oath to serve me, and you've not only betrayed that oath but murdered a loyal soldier of mine. That makes you the lowest form of scum in this kingdom."

"I swore allegiance to you because I had to," Eorin said. "I swore allegiance to this child because I wanted to."

King James didn't respond. He simply raised the Sword of Etossar and swung it. The blade severed Eorin's head from the rest of his body. Christina screamed and tried to charge at the king, but as her hands were tied, she merely fell forward. Her captors grabbed her from behind and propped her back up. The king smirked before taking another drink from the flask.

"Silly girl!" he said. "Don't worry about your friend. The two of you shall be reunited soon." He turned to several soldiers nearby. "Put them into the cage! After I've had my dinner and nap, I shall execute the humans and torture the dwarf until he gives me the information I desire."

The soldiers led the captives out of the encampment. After walking a ways through the trees, Christina spotted a large square cage with iron bars. Four ogres dressed in armor stood around it. One of them opened the door, and the captives were shoved inside. After the ogre closed and locked the door, the soldiers returned to the camp.

CHAPTER TEN
THE ATTACK

The makeshift prison was large enough for Christina and the others to move around in, but this was little comfort. She walked to a corner of the cage, lowered her head, and wept. Gilfoit soon came over and put his arm around her.

"Don't cry for Eorin, child," he said soothingly. "His problems are over. We have our own to worry about."

Christina responded with heaving sobs. Sir Owenday was weeping, too.

"I must say, I was wrong about him," Gilfoit continued. "I thought he would renounce you and tell the king that he was coerced into joining the company. But he was a noble human. He would have made a great Order member, and that's the highest compliment I can bestow upon anyone."

"If I had listened to you and flown to the mountains, Eorin might still be alive. And now the rest of us are going to die, too."

"Let's not dwell on what might have been," Gilfoit replied. "Eorin begged you to take him along. He has proven his worth by serving you to the end. And don't be disheartened by our present circumstances. We may get out of this yet. I've been in worse situations with other children from the World Below."

Christina stopped crying. "You have?"

He nodded.

"If I'm killed, what will happen to the Cycle?"

Gilfoit shrugged. "Boriandar will fetch another child. But you won't die. Take heart and things will turn for the better."

"I want to go home," Christina sniffed. 'I don't like this quest anymore."

"I understand," Gilfoit said in a sympathetic voice. "It's natural for children from your world to feel this way when they're in danger. But it'll pass."

Suddenly the prisoners heard King James cry out, "Where's my venison?"

They looked through the trees toward the encampment and saw the king in the torchlight. He was sitting in his chair again and drinking from the flask. Several frightened servants stood around him, and Christina spotted a large table with rows of dishes heaped high with food.

"Your Majesty," one of the servants said in a terrified voice. "The hunters couldn't fetch any deer for you because they're too difficult to kill in this forest. Perhaps they could find something else?"

The king suddenly tipped the table over, sending plates and silverware cascading to the ground. "I want venison!" he shouted. "I'll have the hunters executed for their incompetence!"

Without any warning, he pulled out his sword and beheaded the nearest servant. Christina screamed and turned away. The murder seemed to calm the king's rage. He scabbarded the Sword and said, "Take away the corpse, clean up this mess, and prepare another meal. And summon my jester to me."

The other servants nearly fell over each other in their efforts to obey him. A few moments later, a small, skinny man in a purple-and-green polka dot suit and cone-shaped hat came somersaulting into view. When he stopped before the king, the man stood up, trembling with fear.

"Belatro, I wish to be entertained," King James said before taking another drink of the Elixir.

"Y-yes, Your Majesty," the jester squeaked. He spent the next several minutes performing magic tricks and juggling fruit before the king finally waved him away. When a new feast was ready, King James devoured his food and then retired to his tent. By that time, the ogres guarding the prisoners had fallen asleep; their snores caused the cage bars to rattle. The prisoners sat down and tried to make themselves comfortable. Sobbing, Christina laid her head on Gilfoit's shoulder and grimly reflected on her situation. She had to admit to herself that while living with Mom in Grand Rapids and going to middle school had been bad, being locked in a cage and awaiting execution was *definitely* worse.

After a while, her thoughts were interrupted by a tap on her shoulder. Turning her head, she expected to see one of the king's soldiers. Instead, a familiar green face stared at her in the dim light.

"Eelweed!" she whispered in joyful surprise. The others turned their heads and gasped when they saw the water gnome.

"Are we happy to see you!" Gilfoit said.

"How did you get all the way out here?" Christina asked.

"I've been following you from afar," Eelweed replied.

"Were you the one who stepped on those twigs that one night we were sitting around the fire?" Gilfoit asked.

Eelweed nodded. "Child, why didn't you tell me you were the new queen?" he asked.

She motioned toward the bars of the cage. "I didn't want anything like this to happen. Gilfoit told me to hide my real identity from strangers. A lot of good that did. I got caught anyway, and Eorin is dead."

"I'm sorry to hear that," Eelweed replied in a solemn voice.

"Well, it looks as though we were right to reject your pleas to join our company," Gilfoit said. "You can now help us escape."

"Oh, will you let us out, please?" Christina asked.

"Of course I will," Eelweed replied.

"But how are you going to get the key?" Sir Owenday asked. "I don't think you want to risk waking up those ogres. They'll squash you into the earth."

"I don't need a key," Eelweed replied. He unstrapped his harpoon and thrust the pointed end into the lock. After jiggling the blade around for several seconds, the lock clicked. He pulled the harpoon out and opened the door before cutting the prisoners' binds with his sword.

"Let's go," Gilfoit said.

"And be quiet, all of you," Sir Owenday whispered. "If there's one thing I've learned in my travels, it's that one must never wake a sleeping ogre, especially if it's hungry."

The company moved away from the slumbering guards and crept through the trees in single file. Christina was having difficulty seeing, for the only source of light came from the bonfire in the king's encampment.

"How are we going to find our way through this place?" she whispered.

Gilfoit pulled his medallion from his cloak. "This should give us some light," he replied, holding it up. "I'd better lead the way."

After they walked about a hundred paces, the company heard an ear-splitting roar. Christina jumped.

"What was that?" she asked in a terrified whisper.

"The ogres!" Eelweed said. "They've awoken and discovered your absence!"

Gilfoit shook his head. "That was no ogre. It sounded like a bear. Let's get far away from here!"

They ran without paying any attention to where they were going and soon heard more terrible roars accompanied by screams from the glade and the swooshing of arrows. Christina, who was right behind Gilfoit, saw him disappear suddenly. A second later, she fell down a ravine with her companions tumbling after her. When they all reached the bottom, she was thankful she hadn't been crushed to death. Gilfoit asked if everyone else was all right, and after the others answered in the affirmative, they started running again. But before the company could go any further, several shadowy figures appeared from all sides and grabbed them.

CHAPTER ELEVEN
LORD BODWAR

Christina struggled to free herself, but strong enormous hands held her in place. It was too dark to see, for Gilfoit had hastily concealed his glowing medallion in the moment of their capture. But before he did so, she caught a glimpse of their captors—nine-foot, human-like creatures dressed in black cloaks. They carried wooden pikes measuring about twenty feet in length, and their dark green faces wore stoic expressions. These creatures had to be waulds, hardly a comforting thought.

Christina heard the terrible screams of King James's men and wondered if she and her companions were going to share a similar grisly fate. When the noise finally stopped, specks of light appeared in the darkness. As they drew closer, she saw tree gnomes carrying torches. In physical appearance, they resembled Eelweed, except they had human-like feet and hair and lacked gills, while leaves covered their bodies in lieu of clothes. One of them held his torch up to her face and yelled, "Helvondir, there's a human girl here! I think it's *her!*"

When the tree gnome named Helvondir came over, Christina saw two familiar figures on his shoulder.

"Sir Kranwick! Crossander!" she cried out in delightful surprise.

"Good evening, Your Majesty," the purple glass knight said. "It pleases me greatly to see you alive and in good health. Master Helvondir, this is Christina of the World Below, and there's Gilfoit and Sir Owenday. I don't know who that water gnome is though."

"I'm Eelweed."

Sir Kranwick nodded. "Pleased to make your acquaintance, sir. Where's Eorin?"

"He's dead," Christina said, closing her eyes for a moment. "King James killed him."

"A great loss, indeed," Sir Kranwick sighed. "I rather liked the human, even though he wasn't a knight."

Helvondir turned to the first tree gnome and said, "Birchmindor, go to Lord Bodwar and tell him that we have the girl."

"Excuse me, but can you find my schoolbag?" Christina asked. "One of our human captors took it." After she described the bag to Birchmindor, he nodded and walked away, his torch flickering through the trees. Helvondir ordered the waulds to release the prisoners.

"How did you find us, Sir Kranwick?" Sir Owenday asked.

"I didn't," the glass knight replied. "The tree gnomes found you."

"Not long ago, we received word that the king was leading an expedition through the forest," Helvondir said. "But we didn't know the new ruler had arrived until this knight came to our tree village a few hours ago and asked for assistance."

Christina looked at Sir Kranwick. "Thank you so much!" she said. "We thought you had abandoned us when we were captured."

"A true knight *never* abandons his comrades," he said loftily after Gilfoit, Sir Owenday, and Eelweed expressed their gratitude. "And your words of thanks are greatly accepted and appreciated."

Soon, more torch-bearing tree gnomes approached, and these were led by a man in a brown fur cloak.

Birchmindor pointed at Christina and said, "There she is, my lord." He handed the girl her schoolbag, and she thanked him. The man came before her and went down on one knee.

"Lord Bodwar, at your service," he said. "Welcome to Ferncandell Forest."

"I'm Christina," she replied, unable to keep her eyes off of the wild black beard that nearly touched the ground. "Thank you for rescuing us."

He rose and said, "I did nothing more than my duty. After all, you're my new queen."

"But you could've sided with King James if you'd wanted to," Christina replied. She marveled at Lord Bodwar's height and build. He was as tall and wide as a tree, and when he stood, she had to tilt her head up in order to look him in the face.

"Never!" he cried. "I despise him beyond all measure! The day he's finally overthrown will be a great one for our kingdom."

After everyone else in the company introduced themselves, Christina said, "What happened to the king and his men?"

"They were treated to a little surprise," Lord Bodwar replied, a wicked grin on his face. "Most of them fled like cowards, but we killed a fair number. Come and see for yourself."

He led everyone back to the glade. The ground was strewn with the remains of the encampment and the corpses of humans and creatures. Some of the abandoned tents still stood. Waulds and tree gnomes searched the corpses for valuables. Christina saw the bodies of Gorgrin and the other bounty seekers who had captured her, but she couldn't find Eorin's remains.

"Lord Bodwar, King James killed one of our friends," she said. "His name was Eorin and he saved my life. Can you help us find his remains? He should get a proper burial."

Lord Bodwar nodded. "If his body is still here, then we shall find it."

After ordering the waulds to carry the corpses away, he helped Christina search for Eorin. They soon found his head and body in the king's tent. She couldn't bear to touch these, so Lord Bodwar carried them outside. She guessed King James had planned to put Eorin's head on display as a warning to any who might oppose him, and this infuriated her.

Helvondir produced a spade and dug a shallow grave. When it was ready, Lord Bodwar placed Eorin's remains inside with a great deal of tenderness. After Helvondir filled the hole with dirt and made a little barrow, Sir Owenday fetched a sword and thrust the blade through the top of the burial mound as a sign of tribute. The company held a quick funeral with Gilfoit, Sir Owenday, and Sir Kranwick making complimentary remarks about the deceased. Christina tried to speak, but a lump in her throat prevented any sound from coming out. The day's events crashed over her like a wave, and she couldn't stop trembling. Tears ran down her face. Eelweed put his arm around her.

"There, there, child," he said kindly. "Eorin's death was a great tragedy, but crying isn't going to bring him back."

"H-he was so nice to me," Christina sobbed.

"Just remember that King James is to blame for this, not you," Gilfoit said. "And the sooner we defeat him, the sooner we can put an end to these injustices."

Sniffling, Christina nodded. Lord Bodwar strode up to her and said, "Sir Owenday here tells me that you need to reach the Mironan Mountains."

"There's a refuge I'm supposed to go to," she said, wiping her face. "Could you help us get to the grassland of Morlinduhl?"

"I can do better than that," he replied. "I shall accompany you to the mountains. If the king's men find you and your friends again, they shan't have an easy go of it."

"Thank you for the offer, but what about your home?"

"It'll still be here when I return."

She was glad to hear this, for she felt safe around Lord Bodwar. "Is it true you can turn into a bear whenever you feel like it? I heard a bear's roar when you attacked the camp."

He nodded. "I usually go into battle as a bear. My hide can deflect many arrows, and I have the strength of a hundred men."

Suddenly, they heard a noise coming from a nearby shrub. Helvondir rushed over and pulled out a short man in a disheveled suit and cone-shaped hat. He held the Sword of Etossar and a black leather scabbard in his right hand.

"That's the king's jester!" Christina said.

"Kill him," Lord Bodwar said to Helvondir.

"Wait!" the jester cried, running up to Christina and kneeling before her. "I wish to join you! Don't let them kill me! I'm not a bad person!"

"Then why do you work for the king?" she asked. "Did you choose to, or were you forced to?"

"Both, to be precise," the little man replied, tears rolling down his cheeks. "Let me explain. Folks call me 'Belatro', and I come from an ancient line of thieves. My father was a thief, his father was a thief, and *his* father—"

"Yes, yes, we understand," Gilfoit growled impatiently. "Get on with it!"

"Yes, sir," the jester squeaked. "I was expected to follow in my father's footsteps. But when I was a young lad, I realized that I possessed a talent for entertaining people, and I loved doing it. Well, father and I had a falling out over this, and he cast me from his home. I wandered the kingdom and earned my daily bread by performing in front of audiences, but it was tough going until I caught the eye of one of King James's courtiers. He brought me to the Amber Castle, and after I entertained His Majesty, he made me his court jester. At first, I loved the job and was given plenty to eat and a comfortable bed to sleep in. I'd heard stories about King James's cruelty but refused to believe them. However, after I saw His Majesty kill

71

several human children who had trespassed in his gardens, I attempted to leave the castle, but his guards caught me, and the king threatened to have me executed if I did that again. Now that I'm finally free of him, I'd like to join you folks and serve this child who has come from the Well."

"If that's true, then why didn't you try to rescue her earlier?" Sir Owenday asked.

"I couldn't leave the glade without arousing suspicion," Belatro squeaked. "King James always keeps me close at hand. But when we were attacked, I stole the sword and hid in this shrub. I may not have chosen the burglar's profession, but I still possess my forefathers' talent for that line of work." Holding the sword out to Christina, he said, "I offer this to you now as proof of my loyalty. Let me be your jester. I can provide your daily amusement, and I'm also a great pickpocket."

"We don't require a thief or a licensed fool," Eelweed replied harshly.

"But you don't know that!" Belatro said. "One or both may come in handy someday."

Christina turned to Gilfoit. "What do you think?"

"I'm not certain that he's reliable," the dwarf replied slowly. "True, he stole the sword for you, but he could have done it in order to buy your trust for his own ends. He may betray you at the first opportunity. That being said, I *was* wrong about Eorin, so perhaps I'm wrong about this fellow as well."

Belatro clasped his hands together. "I'm not a danger to you! Please believe me!"

Moved by the jester's pitiful plea, Christina took the Sword and scabbard and said, "Very well, Belatro. You can join us. But if you commit any treachery, I won't be able to protect you from my friends."

The jester grabbed her free hand and showered it with sloppy kisses while muttering, "Thank you! *Thank you!*"

After a great deal of effort, Christina managed to pull her wet hand away. "That's enough. You're welcome."

"You all should get some rest now," Lord Bodwar said. "We'll leave at first light."

CHAPTER TWELVE
JOURNEY THROUGH THE GRASSLAND

After everyone awoke the next morning, they ate a breakfast of porridge provided by the tree gnomes. Then Lord Bodwar filled a sack with food and waterskins and led Christina, Gilfoit, Sir Owenday, Sir Kranwick, Eelweed, and Belatro out of the forest. When they reached the border, they saw grassland that seemed to stretch into eternity. The ground was level for miles around, but hills and plateaus rose in the distance.

"Here we are!" Lord Bodwar said grandly. "I give you the Grassland of Morlinduhl!"

"Which way do we go?" Christina asked.

"The Mironan Mountains are just ahead," Gilfoit said. "If we keep going straight, we should reach them in a few days."

"Keep your weapons ready," Lord Bodwar said. "We may run into the king's men. Or something worse."

With this warning, the company entered the grassland. After a while, Christina saw a herd of horses

74

in the distance. They all wore stripes of every color and were the most beautiful horses she had ever laid eyes on.

"Look!" she said, pointing at the exotic animals. "What are they?"

"Rainbow mares," Sir Owenday replied casually.

"I've never seen animals that lovely before!" she said.

"Just wait until you've traveled through more of the kingdom," said the horseless knight. "You'll encounter beasts much more beautiful than those horses."

***

As the travelers made their way across the flat grass, Gilfoit walked beside her and said, "How are you holding up, child?"

"Fine," she replied. "Hey Gil, do you know anything about King James's life before he came to Imar?"

"Yes. His parents were killed in an accident, and he went to live with his relations. Apparently, they were unkind to him, and he ran away."

For the first time since her arrival in Imar, Christina felt pity for her enemy. This made her feel uncomfortable because she wanted to continue hating him for what he had done.

"What's it like to be immortal?" she asked, changing the subject. "Do you miss your family?"

"I was orphaned at a very young age and never knew any of my kinfolk," Gilfoit replied. "The same is true for the other Order members. We've all become each other's family. And we enjoy our immortality."

"What will you guys do after King James is overthrown and killed?"

"We'll return to the Sanctuary until the Elixir darkens again."

"Don't you guys get tired of doing this over and over?"

Gilfoit shrugged. "We're accustomed to the Cycle. But when the Eternal Ruler reveals himself, or herself, we Order members can leave the Sanctuary and live wherever we wish in eternal peace."

"I don't understand something. Why did Ethindir make it possible for the Well to be destroyed? Why didn't he just let the Cycle go on forever?"

"He was a deeply enigmatic figure who didn't often give reasons for his actions. But he erred in believing that no one can wield absolute power forever without being corrupted. I'm certain that if Ethindir had lived to hear the Prophecy, he would never have made it possible for the Well to be destroyed."

Christina grew silent. She wondered if she would turn out to be the person Lord Evermore's prophecy spoke of. Probably not. But *maybe*. The kingdom had been waiting eight thousand years for the Eternal Ruler to arrive; surely, the time had come. Gilfoit had said that this child would not be like the others. Hadn't *she* always been different from the other kids in her own world?

Back in Grand Rapids, Christina liked to believe that she was a special person with a great destiny. Such musings often provided her with an escape—albeit a temporary one—from her dreary life. The events of the past week only served to reinforce this belief, and the idea that she might fulfill an age-old prophecy slowly began to overcome her initial doubts about remaining in the kingdom upon completion of her quest.

***

The company traveled through the grassland during the day and rested at night. By the fourth day, Christina began experiencing the overwhelming sense of tedium that had plagued her during much of the journey through Ferncandell Forest. But whereas the forest had at least offered some amazing sights, the Grassland of Morlinduhl seemed, for the most part, to be a pretty dull and desolate place; she hadn't seen any other creatures besides the rainbow mares and some moles with silver fur. Her legs ached, and the intense heat caused streams of sticky sweat to run down her body. Christina's discomfort was exacerbated by the fact that the leather scabbard, which held the Sword of Etossar and hung from the belt given to her by Gilfoit, flopped against her leg as she walked.

Although she took great pains to conceal her exhaustion, Christina's face betrayed her inner feelings. As the company made its way through a series of high hills blanketed by short yellow grass, Lord Bodwar came up beside her and said, "Child, you look tired. Why don't you ride upon my back?"

"I'd like that," she said. "But it wouldn't be fair of me to get a ride while the others have to walk."

"How considerate of you," he replied. "But I can carry others as well."

"Alright," Christina said. "I'd love to have a ride. Thank you."

"My pleasure. Would anyone else like to ride upon my back? The only thing I ask in return is that one of you watches my sack."

"I would," Belatro said. "And I can look after your sack."

Lord Bodwar transformed into a bear, and Christina and Belatro mounted his back. She felt much better, for the shape-shifter provided a smooth and comfortable ride. As the company crested a steep hill, Eelweed pointed at a series of jagged gray peaks far ahead and shouted, "Look! There are the mountains!"

"Don't get too excited," Gilfoit said. "We still have a ways to go."

Christina looked down, and something caught her eye. About thirty feet from the bottom of the hill was a deep oval-shaped basin filled with flowers. Each flower had silver, gold, and ruby petals. A strange sense of longing suddenly seized her, and she jumped off Lord Bodwar's back and descended the hill before anyone could stop her. Halfway down, she slipped on a tuft of grass and rolled to the bottom. Rising quickly, she ran to the basin, flung herself into the flowers, and inhaled their heavenly fragrance. The others soon joined her. She pulled a handful of flowers from the ground and held them up.

"Look what I have!" she cried. "Have you ever seen anything so beautiful? What kind of flowers are these?"

"I don't know," Gilfoit replied. "Christina, you should be more careful."

"I couldn't help it," she said.

"We should leave," Sir Owenday said. "Something about this place feels wrong to me."

"Oh, let's stay a few minutes longer!" she said, taking another deep sniff.

"I think Sir Owenday is right," Gilfoit said. "Don't you, Lord Bodwar?" He turned to the bear, only to find him, Sir Kranwick, and Crossander fast asleep.

Sir Owenday gave a deep yawn. "I'm…very …tired. Let's just…rest here…a while…" He lay on the ground and began snoring loudly.

"I feel tired, too," Belatro said.

"So do I," Eelweed added.

"You all get some rest," Gilfoit said, yawning. "I'll…stand…" His voice trailed off, and he collapsed on the ground. For a few minutes, Christina struggled to stay awake, but she, too, fell asleep.

***

A few hours later, a loud hissing sound woke her up, and she felt something icy around her neck. When she opened her eyes, she screamed in terror. A woman wearing a translucent yellow gown was attempting to strangle her. She had an angelic face, but her mouth contorted into a malevolent grin, displaying rows of dark jagged teeth. Through her peripheral vision, Christina noticed that dense, high grass now surrounded the basin. Her screams startled the strange woman, who pulled her hands away.

"Leave me alone!" Christina cried, standing up and drawing the Sword of Etossar. The woman gave an ear-splitting shriek and glided away. Christina looked back at her friends and discovered, to her surprise, that the commotion hadn't roused any of them from their slumber. She climbed out of the basin and walked several feet into the high grass. Then her foot hit something. Looking down, she saw a human skeleton lying on the ground.

Christina screamed, ran back into the basin, and tried to wake her companions, to no avail. She shook them as hard as she could, but they seemed to be in some kind of enchanted sleep. She spent several minutes slapping Eelweed in the face in a desperate attempt to pull him out of his slumber, and to her great relief, he finally gave a muffled groan and sat up.

"Where am I?" he asked groggily.

"You're still in the basin," Christina said in a frantic voice. "But we've moved somehow. There's tall grass everywhere."

He stared around with a stupid look on his face. "We had best wake our friends. Perhaps one of them will know a way out of this."

The two of them shook the others until they came to. After Christina showed everyone the skeleton and told them about the woman who attacked her, Gilfoit said, "We must be in the Goulind Plain. That's what they call the center of Morlinduhl. It's flat land with high grass for miles in every direction. This basin must have moved here by means of some powerful magic, and I'm not certain as to how we can leave."

"Can't we just walk out of here?" Christina asked.

"We can try," Sir Owenday replied. "But folks say you can't get out of the Goulind Plain alive unless you have a flying beast. There's some dark enchantment in this place that prevents travelers from finding a way out. Compasses and other means of discerning direction won't work here. More likely than not, we'll end up going around in circles until we die of hunger or thirst."

"Well, we're in a pretty spot," Eelweed grumbled.

"There is a bright side to this," Belatro said in an attempt to lift everyone's spirits. "The king and his men will *never* find Christina in here."

The others shook their heads in exasperation.

"I don't mind dying," Sir Kranwick said gloomily as Sir Owenday gently picked him and Crossander up and put them on his shoulder. "I only wish I could have done so on the field of battle. Now I'll never reach Aressindor."

"Are there friendly creatures here that could help us?" Christina asked.

Gilfoit shook his head. "I don't think so. This place is pretty isolated. We're not likely to encounter anyone here, at least not anyone friendly."

"Well, that's just great!" she said. "What are we going to do? We'll never get to the mountains!"

"We mustn't lose hope," Lord Bodwar said. "Let's continue our journey and see if we can't stumble upon a way out of this place."

"I'll go first and clear a path for the rest of you," Gilfoit said, pulling out a short sword.

Walking through the high grass, the company came across the remains of other unfortunate wayfarers. As morning gave way to noon, the heat grew insufferable. Finally, Gilfoit said, "We have to rest. It won't do us any good to walk until we drop dead of exhaustion."

He and Sir Owenday hacked away at the grass with their swords and made a little clearing. The company sat in a circle, and those with food and water shared it with the others. Christina was offered larger portions, but she refused to take more than her companions. When the travelers rose to resume their journey, the ground suddenly started shaking.

"What's that?" she asked in a terrified voice.

"I think it's some kind of herd," Gilfoit replied. "And it sounds like it's coming this way."

Suddenly an animal charged through the grass and tore past the group. To Christina, it looked like a goat with a yellow hide and fearsome swiveling horns shaped like an insect's antennae.

"What kind of a beast was *that?*" Eelweed asked.

"A wild yale," Sir Owenday replied. "They live in certain parts of the grassland."

A second later, another yale came running through the makeshift clearing. Before long, the company found itself in the midst of a large throng. The animals let out a high-pitched bleat that hurt Christina's ears. Lord Bodwar transformed into a man, picked her and Eelweed up, and put them on his broad shoulders while Sir Owenday lifted Gilfoit and Belatro and held them up as high as he could.

"Let's get away from these beasts!" Lord Bodwar cried. "Everyone stay close!"

The group moved leftward and tried to make their way toward the outer edge of the herd, but this proved a daunting challenge. The yales were tightly packed together, allowing only a few small gaps here and there. Suddenly, a large yale hit Lord Bodwar in the side of the leg. He lurched forward, and Christina slipped from his shoulder and landed on the back of another yale. She grabbed the animal's neck with both hands and screamed in terror as it carried her farther and farther away from her friends. The animal tried to shake her off, but she held on with a viselike grip and stayed clear of its horns.

Before long, Christina's arms grew tired. Every second felt like agony, but she dared not let go for fear of being trampled by the herd. As grass whipped her in the face, panic set in. She hadn't liked being lost before, but at least she had company. Even if she got away from these yales in one piece, she would never find her friends again.

After a while, Christina heard swooshing sounds above the din of the stampede. Turning her head, she saw several yales buckle and fall to the ground with arrows sticking out of their hides. The herd soon entered a vast clearing, and two short green-skinned people riding what looked like small unicorns appeared off to her right. She took a deep breath and yelled, "Help me!"

Hearing her cry, the people made their way into the herd. But before they could reach her, she lost her grip and fell to the ground. Darkness shrouded her mind.

CHAPTER THIRTEEN
THE GRASS PEOPLE

When Christina awoke, she found herself lying on a bed of fresh grass and coarse brown linen. She sat up and looked around. This took considerable effort, for her body felt stiff. She soon realized that she was in a square hut where the floor, walls, and roof were made of thatched grass. The bed she was lying on rested against one wall while a much larger bed stood against the wall on the opposite end of the hut. A moment later, the door opened and a small yellow-skinned woman in a green dress entered.

"I see you're up," she said in a cheerful voice when she saw Christina. "Would you like some tea?"

Although her throat felt as dry as a desert, Christina hesitated before replying. Her parents had warned her never to accept anything from strangers, and this woman definitely appeared strange. But her maternal smile soon disarmed Christina's suspicions, and she said, "Yes, please."

The woman walked over to a clay stove in the back of the hut, and when she moved, her dress dragged along the ground. As Christina watched her pick up a gray kettle that sat on top of the stove and pour something into a handless cup, she noticed her schoolbag resting on a round table surrounded by three chairs.

The woman handed the cup to Christina, who thanked her. After staring down into the cup and seeing a bile-green liquid with bits of grass floating in it, she closed her eyes and took a cautious drink. To her amazement, the tea had a wonderful spicy taste. She downed the rest of it in one gulp and felt strength returning to her body. The woman smiled and refilled the cup. After Christina drank her fill, her host put the cup on the table, sat in one of the chairs, and stared at the child.

"I don't mean to be rude, but what are you?" Christina asked. Like the other creatures she had encountered in Imar, this woman was exotic, with her elfin face and dark grassy hair.

"Have you never seen a polevick before?"

Christina shook her head.

"My name is Erinonda," the woman said. "My husband and son pulled you out of the yale herd and brought you here. Fortunately, they were able to reach you before you were hurt."

"I'm Christina."

"Pleased to meet you, Christina. You have such a lovely name."

"Thank you. What were your family members riding? Were those unicorns?"

"No, minicorns. Now tell me where you're from, child. What were you doing in the Goulind Plain? That's no place for human children."

Christina was about to answer when she realized that the sword and its scabbard were gone. Then she remembered her friends.

"My sword!" she cried. "Where is it? And my friends! I left them in the tall grass! I need to find them!"

"Don't worry," Erinonda said in a soothing voice. "My husband has your sword. As for your friends, we shall find them in good time. Ah, here come my husband and son now. They'll be glad to see you're awake and well."

A moment later, two polevick men came in accompanied by a strange animal, which looked like a black armadillo with an elephant trunk for a nose. As soon as it entered the hut, the animal scurried over to Christina and began to thrust its long nose against parts of her body. This made her uncomfortable, but she dared not push the animal away for fear of offending its owners.

The men wore green shirts and leggings and brown belts, but nothing on their feet. Each of them carried a small bow and wore a quiver of arrows on his back, while a long curved knife dangled from his belt. One of the men looked fairly old, while the other resembled a teenager.

"The child says her name is Christina," Erinonda said.

"You are welcome in my home," the elderly man said. "My name is Metorah." He stood nearly as tall as Christina, and she admired his wizened beard and noticed that his free hand clutched the Sword of Etossar in its scabbard.

Metorah motioned to the youthful-looking polevick and said, "This is Fryndain, my son."

"Hi," Christina said shyly.

"Hello, human child," Fryndain replied, smiling at her and showing two rows of orange teeth. In contrast to his father, he was completely bald and stood half a foot shorter.

"We are members of the Fragelindor clan," Metorah continued. "I'm the chief. Fryndain and I found the Sword of Etossar on you. How did you come across it? And what part of the kingdom do you hail from?"

Although Gilfoit had warned her not to reveal her identity to strangers, Christina decided to tell these polevicks the truth. "I didn't steal the sword," she said in a tremulous voice. "Somebody else did that. And I'm not from Imar. I came down the Well a few weeks ago."

The polevicks gasped. "Not long ago, we heard that a child had arrived from the World Below," Metorah said. "How did you end up in the Goulind Plain? And can you prove to us that you're the new ruler?"

She nodded. "One of my friends is a member of the Order of Ethindir and wears a medallion that glows when a child from my world is near. We were going through the tall grass when we found ourselves in the middle of the yale herd. I was on Lord Bodwar's shoulder when I fell off and landed on one of the animals. Can you please help me find my friends? They're lost in the tall grass. Please don't hand me over to King James. We need to get to the Mironan Mountains."

"Have no fear," Metorah replied in a kind voice. "Fryndain will take you into the grass and help you find your friends. You can borrow my wife's minicorn. The only thing I ask in return is that your friend with the medallion confirms your status."

"Alright," Christina said. "But how will we find my friends? They're out in the middle of nowhere."

Metorah pointed at the animal, which now buried its long nose in Christina's crotch and sniffed away like a dog.

"Bulda here will do it," he said. "You mentioned before that you were on one of your friends' shoulders. That means his scent is on your body. Bulda will pick it up and track it to the source."

"What kind of animal is he?"

"A terandrick," Metorah said, handing her the Sword and scabbard. "Now go with my son."

***

When Fryndain, Christina, and Bulda left the hut, she saw that they were in a village of grass huts in another large clearing. Other polevicks were out and about, and they stared at the girl, which made her feel awkward. Stopping at a nearby stable, Fryndain helped Christina onto Erinonda's minicorn before mounting his own. When the two of them entered the formidable grass, the polevick gave Bulda a command in a strange language. Then the animal tore through the green wilderness with the riders close on his heels. As the minicorns galloped through the high grass, Christina held a hand out in front of her to avoid being whipped in the face again.

After a while, the minicorns slowed to a steady trot, and she turned to Fryndain and asked, "Aren't we going to lose your pet?"

"Oh no," he replied. "He'll be certain not to run too far ahead of us. Now tell me, Christina, how did you end up here?"

So she related the tale of her journey, and when she reached the part about the basin of flowers and the woman with the yellow gown, Fryndain interrupted her and said, "I see you've met a lakanica. They're beautiful but dangerous field spirits who use these basins to trap humans and creatures. We call them lakanica snares. The flowers are enchanted and cast a spell on many who look upon them. And when the victims jump into the snare and inhale the sweet fragrance, they fall asleep. Then they disappear and reappear in another snare in the center of the grassland. When the victims wake up, they're lost, and miles away from any source of help. Once that happens, they usually die of thirst or starvation, and the lakanicas smell the corpses and fly over to feast on their blood. Sometimes they'll even try to strangle their victims if they find them sleeping. It was very fortunate that you woke up when you did."

Christina shuddered. "I'll never go near one of those snares again," she said. "Do all of the polevicks live out here?"

Fryndain shook his head. "Most of the polevick clans reside in the western part of Morlinduhl. But some of us prefer the Goulind Plain because of the peaceful isolation it affords. And the hunting—"

Their conversation was interrupted by Bulda, who made a noise that sounded like a cross between a snort and a squeal.

CHAPTER FOURTEEN
HONORED GUESTS

"He's found something!" Fryndain cried.

The two of them galloped toward the terandrick, and she heard Eelweed say, "What *is* this ugly thing? Go away!"

"Here they are!" Christina shouted. When she saw her friends, she jumped off her minicorn and hugged each of them in turn. "Am I glad to see you guys! Are you all right?"

"We're fine," Gilfoit said, staring down at Bulda with a mixture of curiosity and fear. "What kind of animal is this?"

"A terandrick," she replied. "Don't worry. He's completely harmless, I think. He belongs to this polevick. Meet Fryndain of the Fragelindor clan."

After her friends introduced themselves, Fryndain said, "Christina tells me that one of you has a medallion which proves she's the new queen."

"I have it," Gilfoit replied, pulling his medallion out and holding it toward Christina. When Fryndain saw it glow, he pronounced himself satisfied.

"Thank you for helping me find my friends, Fryndain," Christina said.

"It's my pleasure," he replied. "Now let's return to the village."

***

When the company reached Metorah's hut, the old polevick was sitting on the grass with his wife. While Fryndain took the minicorns into the stable, Christina introduced her friends. Gilfoit pulled his medallion out again to prove Christina's identity, and Metorah nodded. He and Erinonda rose and bowed low before Christina, who blushed in embarrassment.

"Christina of the World Below, it is an honor to have you in our village," Metorah said with reverence. "Now please excuse me while I meet with the other clan elders and discuss our next move. I want to help you and your friends but must obtain support from a majority of the elders before I act on so important a matter. Don't be worried, child. I hold a great deal of sway with the clan council. Everything will work out for the best, I promise you. But this meeting may last a few hours, so Fryndain will keep you and your friends entertained."

After Metorah walked away to collect the other elders, Fryndain turned to the company and said, "Let's have an archery contest to pass the time, shall we? Are any of you skilled with a bow?"

"I'm one of the best archers in the kingdom," Gilfoit replied, puffing his chest out with pride.

"I'm pretty good myself," Sir Owenday said, "Although I'm better with a sword."

"Anyone else?" Fryndain asked, looking around.

When the others shook their heads, he led the company to another hut that served as the clan's armory. Christina saw racks of bows, quivers of arrows, and an assortment of other weapons, including daggers and slingshots. Fryndain handed bows and quivers to Gilfoit and Sir Owenday. Then everyone walked over to a shooting range on the edge of the clearing. A line of square targets stood several hundred yards away.

"First, a contest of speed," Fryndain said. "Let's see how long it takes for you to hit your targets with twenty arrows. Gilfoit, why don't you go first? Then the knight can shoot. I'll go last."

Gilfoit laughed. "Very well," he said. "But I warn you, I'm a quick shot. Hey there, Eelweed. Can you count time for us?"

"Absolutely," the water gnome replied. "Are you ready?"

"Yes."

"Loose!"

Gilfoit shot twenty arrows in a minute, and every one of them hit his target. The others clapped and cheered. Sir Owenday spent more than five minutes hitting his target twenty times with sixty-three of his arrows. This unimpressive showing generated a smattering of polite applause.

Gilfoit grinned at Fryndain. "Well, polevick, it looks like I'm the winner so far," he said.

Fryndain nodded. "You're not bad for an outsider. Ready, timekeeper?"

"Ready," Eelweed replied. "Loose!"

Fryndain yanked arrows out of his quiver and shot them so fast that his actions were a blur to Christina. She barely grasped what was happening when he shouted, "Done! Time?"

"Ten seconds," Eelweed gasped. "That was incredible! I've never seen anything like it!"

"I'll say," Christina said. She looked over at Fryndain's target and was startled to see all of his arrows clustered around the bull's-eye. In contrast, most of his competitors' arrows were wide off the mark.

"That was impressive," Gilfoit said grudgingly. "But let's see who can hit the center of a bull's-eye the most times in a row."

Fryndain flashed a grin. "I was about to suggest that."

"Count me out," Sir Owenday said, his face red with embarrassment.

"I guess it's only you and me now, dwarf," Fryndain said. "Why don't you go first?"

"Don't mind if I do," Gilfoit replied. He walked to a different target and shot an arrow. It hit the center of the bull's-eye. He fit another arrow in his bow, took careful aim, and let fly. This arrow hit the first one and split the shaft apart. Applause and cheers. Gilfoit's third arrow split the second arrow's shaft apart, and this continued until he reached the sixth arrow, which hit a few inches above the others.

"Bravo!" Sir Kranwick cried. "Let's see you beat that, polevick!"

Gilfoit grinned at Fryndain, whose own grin hadn't disappeared.

"That was a marvelous demonstration of archery," the polevick said. "Now it's my turn."

He removed an arrow from his quiver, shot it at another target, and hit the center of the bull's-eye. Then he shot nineteen more arrows with the same skill and speed that he displayed in the earlier contest. Each arrow split open the shaft of the one before it, and when Fryndain finished, Christina saw a series of giant "V's" sticking out of the bull's-eye. Everyone except Gilfoit clapped and cheered madly.

"Show off," the dwarf muttered.

"Can you teach me how to shoot like that?" Christina asked.

Fryndain laughed. "It takes years to learn to shoot a bow expertly, and we polevicks are born archers. But I'll teach you the basics if you like."

And so for the next several hours, he introduced her to the art of archery. Christina had difficulty mastering the bow, and all of her arrows ended up on the ground, but she was having a lot of fun and didn't care about her lack of prowess. She couldn't believe how much time had passed when a young polevick ran up to Fryndain to inform him that Metorah and the elders had concluded their meeting.

***

Fryndain led the company to a circular hut with a domed roof, where Metorah and a group of polevicks were waiting for them outside. Christina felt anxious, but her worries disappeared the moment she saw the broad smile on the clan chief's face. After his peers introduced themselves and bowed to her, Metorah said, "Child, I've discussed your situation with the elders, and they've concurred with my decision to help you reach your destination."

"I don't know how I can ever thank you!" she said.

"I know of a way," he replied. "We would like you and your friends to be our honored guests tonight. It's not often that we have a future ruler amongst us. We'll have a bonfire with feasting and dancing. You can all sleep in our guest hut, and Fryndain and I will take you to the mountains at dawn."

Christina looked at her companions. "What do you think?"

"We should be heading for the Sanctuary right now," Gilfoit said. "We've lost too much time as it is."

"But perhaps another day won't hurt," Lord Bodwar said. "I'm sure all of us are tired and hungry."

The others agreed to this, so Christina accepted Metorah's offer. Word about the guests soon spread among the other Fragelindars, and many of them came to pay homage to Christina. These displays of adulation made her heart swell with pride and delight. She had always wanted to know what it was like to be loved by many people; Christina figured it had to be better than being loved by no one, which is how she always felt back in her own world.

When the sun descended, the polevicks lit a giant bonfire in the middle of the clearing. They roasted several yales and everyone sat on the ground and ate. Christina greedily devoured the tender, juicy meat along with sweet corn on the cob and gulped down cup after cup of tea. She also enjoyed the desserts, which included seed cakes and sugared stalk. During the meal, Metorah, Erinonda, and Fryndain asked Christina about her world, and as they talked, she realized that she liked the polevicks a lot. They were friendly creatures, and the close bond they shared with one another was a pleasant contrast to her own family. Even before the divorce, her parents fought all of the time, causing Christina a great deal of stress and anxiety.

When the feast was over, the guests watched the clan elders perform a ritual dance around the bonfire. After they finished, the polevick children came up to do a dance of their own, and Christina and her friends were invited to participate. At first she tried to refuse, but Fryndain grabbed her arm and pushed her forward. She danced and sang with the children, and it was the most fun she had had in a long time.

After several hours of merriment, Christina felt very tired. She tried to stay awake, but her eyelids soon drooped of their own accord. Strong, gentle hands lifted her up and carried her to a bed of soft grass, where she drifted into a wonderful slumber.

CHAPTER FIFTEEN
THE ORDER OF ETHINDIR

When Fryndain woke Christina the next morning, the sun was creeping over the horizon. After everyone enjoyed a breakfast of seed cakes and roasted yale left over from the feast, Metorah and Fryndain led Christina and her friends into the high grass. By the time the company arrived at the edge of the Goulind Plain, where the grass came up to Christina's waist, she could see the mountains again. Surely, she told herself, it wouldn't be too much longer before they reached them.

Unfortunately, the mountains were further away than she thought. Finally, after several miserable days of traveling through humid weather and heavy rain, the company came to the foot of the Mironan range and spotted a dozen men and dwarfs flying toward them on griffins.

"Soldiers of the king?" Eelweed asked, grabbing his sword.

Gilfoit fitted an arrow to his bow. Then he squinted and said, "There's Albrik! Those are members of the Order!"

When the griffins landed in front of the company, Christina saw that their riders were dressed in silver cloaks except for the leader of the group, who wore gold. The leader, a man, looked tall and stoic, and his snow-white hair flowed down to his shoulders.

"Greetings, Gilfoit," he said in a majestic voice. After surveying the others, he looked down upon the girl. "Is this the child we've all been waiting for?"

"Yes," Gilfoit replied. "Christina, this is Lord Evermore, Head of the Order of Ethindir. Lord Evermore, meet Christina of the World Below."

Lord Evermore bowed his head and said, "Welcome."

Christina was so taken aback by his impressive appearance and commanding presence that she couldn't speak. Finally, after an insufferable moment, she managed to squeak out a "hello."

"Lord Evermore, how did you know we were coming today?" Gilfoit asked.

"I didn't," he replied. "Albrik gave me your message, but by that time, the king had already learned of the child's presence. So I sent Albrik to find the child and make sure she was well. I'm thankful that you decided to travel on foot, for you might have been caught had you flown. Fortunately, much of the kingdom is now in rebellion, so King James has been compelled to divert many of his soldiers away from his search. I've been circling these mountains for the past several days in the hope that you would arrive. Did you encounter the king or his men? My scouts reported that he was leading an expedition south of here."

Gilfoit nodded and motioned toward the others. "His bounty seekers found us in Ferncandell Forest and took us to the king, but we were rescued by Lord Bodwar here. And these polevicks gave us food and shelter and guided us through the grassland."

"The Order of Ethindir is indebted to you," Lord Evermore said. "But who are these other four that accompany the child?"

Gilfoit quickly introduced the rest of the company and said, "They support the queen."

"Very well," Lord Evermore replied. "But we have the child now and will fly her to the Sanctuary. Those of you not in the Order may take your leave."

"That is well," Metorah said. "Fryndain and I must return to our village."

"Metorah, can you guide me back to the forest?" Lord Bodwar asked. "I mean to return to my home."

"I shall require guidance through the grassland as well," Sir Kranwick said. "I must go to Ifartheon and ready my army for war."

The clan chief assented to these requests and asked if anyone else wished to get across the grassland.

"I shall remain with the child," Sir Owenday said. "She has chosen me to be her bodyguard."

After Christina's other friends expressed a desire to stay with her, Lord Evermore said, "I'm sorry, but the rest of you can't come to the Sanctuary. Nobody but Order members and future rulers are allowed to enter."

Although Christina had finally reached safety, the idea of parting with Sir Owenday, Eelweed, and Belatro made her very uncomfortable. During the course of her journey, they had become close friends, and she realized that she couldn't leave them, especially if they wanted to remain with her.

"I want my friends to come with me," she said to Lord Evermore. "And I'm not going any further unless they do."

"You can trust us," Eelweed said. "We're as dedicated to the child's well-being as you are."

"That's right," Belatro added.

"You've heard my decision," Christina said firmly as she looked the Head of the Order directly in the eye. "Let them come or go away."

"I think we'll be fine, leader," Gilfoit said. "I'll vouch for the child's friends, and they'll be under our control."

"Very well," Lord Evermore replied reluctantly. "You friends of Christina may come to our refuge. Now we must leave at once. You can all ride with an Order member."

After saying goodbye to Lord Bodwar, Metorah, Fryndain, and Sir Kranwick, the rest of Christina's companions mounted griffins. But she didn't move. Instead, she looked down at Sir Kranwick and said, "Thank you for your help."

"It was my pleasure, Your Majesty," he replied. "Thank you for giving us miniatures the chance to finally go to war."

Christina nodded. "I'll return to Ifartheon with my army, and we'll go to the Amber Castle together."

"Please don't do that!" Sir Kranwick said. "We miniatures don't like it when large crowds of humans and creatures come into our land because they cause all kinds of damage. Our army will meet you at the castle. I promise."

"It's a deal," Christina said before turning to Lord Bodwar and giving him a bear hug. "Thank you, too."

"You're very welcome, child," he said. "Good luck. Till we meet again."

She tried to hug Metorah and Fryndain, but they bristled at this gesture of affection, which was foreign to their ways. They gave a solemn bow, which she returned.

"Farewell, Christina," Metorah said. "May you triumph over the king."

"Thank you," she said. "Will I ever see you two again?"

"Perhaps," he replied. "We Fragelindars usually stay in the Goulind Plain, but we may visit the Amber Castle after you take the throne."

"I'd love that. Thank you for your help."

"There is nothing to thank," he said kindly. "We consider you a part of our family now."

Tears of joy sprang to Christina's eyes when she heard this. After she said a final goodbye, Lord Evermore helped her climb on his flying beast, and the griffins took off into the air.

CHAPTER SIXTEEN
LORD EVERMORE

At first, Christina was afraid of flying so high, but she soon overcame this fear and enjoyed herself.

"Your griffin is lovely," she said, admiring the smooth white head in front of her. "What's its name, and is it a male or female?"

"Taris," Lord Evermore replied. "He's a male."

"Can I have a griffin when I become queen?"

"Oh no, child. You can have something much more beautiful. Do you know what an empyremare is?"

Christina shook her head.

"It's a flying unicorn. Only rulers are allowed to have those."

"Really?" She furrowed her brow. "But when we were taken to King James's encampment, I didn't see an empyremare."

"He has one named Mirabol," Lord Evermore replied. "He usually keeps her at the Amber Castle."

"Oh. Where do empyremares come from?"

"In the skies above these mountains lies the celestial country of Ivenara, home of the celestonirs. They're the ones who breed and raise the empyremares."

"When do I get mine?"

"All in good time."

After a minute of silence, Christina asked, "How did you get to be the Head of the Order and what did you do before you joined?"

"When I was a small boy, the ruler was a corrupt and violent king named Landar," Lord Evermore replied. "My father was a famous seer who supported the rebels in our fiefdom, and he predicted the date of Landar's death. Before long, news of this prediction spread throughout the kingdom. When the king learned of it, he sent men to my father's house, and they murdered him and my mother right before my eyes. I was then taken from my home and raised by one of the king's servants. When I came of age, I was conscripted into Landar's army. Before long, I showed an ability to lead others and quickly rose through the ranks to become an important commander. I also established a reputation as a great seer in my own right, for I had inherited my father's gift."

He paused for several moments before continuing. "But I never forgot what the king's minions did to my parents, and I vowed revenge. After I was made a general, I deserted the army and led the rebellion shortly before Ethindir came down from the mountains and killed Landar on the very day my father had prophesied. As it happened, Ethindir was in the process of establishing the Cycle of Royal Succession and offered me leadership of the Order; I accepted without hesitation. Since then, I have striven to rid this kingdom of evil."

"Wow, that's a great story," Christina said. She then lapsed into silence and admired the craggy snow-capped peaks silhouetted against the morning sun. As she stared down at the yawning valleys peppered with trees and the narrow passes that wound their way through the vast, high, rocky wilderness, she thought about the Sanctuary and wondered what it would look like; it was probably nothing more than a series of dank, dark caverns.

"Where's the Sanctuary?" she asked.

"Far beneath the peak of Etossar, which lies in the center of the Mironan range," Lord Evermore replied.

"Isn't that where Ethindir used to live?"

He nodded. "There are seven passageways that lead down to it. Only we Order members know their locations."

"What if King James's men find them by accident?"

"That's nigh impossible, and besides, a passageway can't be opened without an ouroboros medallion. Rulers have tried to capture an Order member in the hope of entering the Sanctuary, but they have never been successful. We are extremely careful and highly skilled in arms."

"How long will I have to stay in the Sanctuary?"

"Perhaps a week or so. Soon the entire kingdom will turn against King James. Then we'll leave the Sanctuary, recruit a large army, and take the Amber Castle in a decisive victory."

"Will I have to lead the attack?" Christina asked apprehensively.

Lord Evermore laughed. "Of course not! You won't be in the fighting. The last thing we need is for you to be killed storming the castle. We Order members don't participate in the battles of royal succession, either. We're too important."

Christina was relieved. Back in Grand Rapids, she had loved pretending to fight in battle, but the real thing scared her to death.

***

After several hours of flying, she needed to pee, but—afraid of sounding childish—she dared not say anything. Before long, the company approached a wide, deep gully blanketed by red grass, and Lord Evermore directed his griffin to fly down there. The rest of the griffins followed suit, and the company landed next to the gully wall. Without dismounting, Lord Evermore pulled his medallion out and pressed it against the smooth gray stone. Christina gasped as she watched millions of tiny yellow crystals appear on the wall and form a massive glittering door, which towered over the company. Sitting in front of it, she felt as small as Sir Kranwick.

As Lord Evermore put his medallion back inside his cloak, the crystals disappeared and revealed an enormous tunnel sloping downward. The griffins flapped their wings, and as soon as they flew into the tunnel, the yellow crystals disappeared and were replaced by stone. But more of these crystals dotted the ceiling, providing light. The musty air rushed past the company as the griffins flew several miles down into the subterranean world. The beasts made many sharp turns, and at certain points during the journey, Christina thought she would crash into the wall. This ride felt like a rough and scary rollercoaster, and she yearned for a seat belt or safety bar as she swiftly descended into the bowels of the Mironan Mountains and was jerked right and left.

At last, the griffins landed in a clean, narrow chamber carved out of purple granite. After the flight through the twisting tunnel, Christina felt nauseated. Looking over at one end of the chamber, she saw an oval door made from thousands of the yellow crystals, with six caverns branching off on either side of it. As the company approached the enchanted door, the crystals dissolved and revealed a low, level tunnel.

The griffins trotted down the tunnel and carried their passengers into another chamber, this one vast, round, and carved out of crimson marble. The wall stood several hundred feet, and white crystals crisscrossed the arched ceiling in long flickering lines. A wide curved staircase snaked its way up the wall to the top of the chamber, and corridor entrances were placed along this winding route at various points. In the middle of the floor stood a white circular fountain with a statue of a man resting on its base. He had a flowing beard, wore a cloak, and carried a long staff. Christina knew this man could be none other than the great sorcerer Ethindir.

"Here we are, Christina," Lord Evermore said. "This will be your home for the time being. Do you have any questions?"

For a moment, she didn't answer but stared with wonder at the Sanctuary. But as she listened to the soft, steady trickling of the water in the fountain, it reminded her of the one thing that had been pressing on her mind.

"Where's your bathroom?"

Chapter Seventeen
The Greatest Weapon

The Sanctuary contained hundreds of rooms, and Christina, Sir Owenday, Eelweed, and Belatro explored every one of them. Most of these were small and unoccupied, but among the larger ones, they discovered a library, a kitchen, an armory, and a main hall for meetings, meals, and ceremonies. All of the corridors were connected to one another, and several of them led to an area of gardens, streams, lakes, fields, valleys, and little farms where animals were raised for food and travel. In this part of the Sanctuary, blue crystals covered the ceiling, which lay several hundred feet above the ground and created a feeling of being outside.

Christina's bedchamber had a comfortable canopy bed, a giant arched mirror, a table and chairs, and a black wardrobe filled with clothes provided by the Order. At first, it felt strange wearing tabards, surcoats, tunics, and other unfamiliar items, but she soon grew used to these. To her shock, the humans in this kingdom were unfamiliar with underwear, and she was thankful she had packed five pairs before leaving home.

On her second day in the Sanctuary, Sir Owenday broached the subject of sword training at dinnertime.

"Christina would you like me to teach you to wield a blade?" he asked. "You may never need to use your sword, but it can't hurt to be prepared. I can start training you tomorrow morning if you like."

"I'd love to have you teach me!" she said excitedly.

That night in her bed, Christina lay awake thinking about how great it would be if she turned out to be a sword fighting prodigy like the heroes in her favorite stories. But by the next morning, the excitement had worn off and a pessimistic reality set in. Why did she ever think she could handle a sword when she couldn't even serve a volleyball in gym class? Likely, she would make a fool of herself, and Sir Owenday would tell the others. Then they would all laugh at her, just like the kids at school. Should she pretend to be sick? No, if she was going to face humiliation, better to get it over with.

After breakfast the next morning, Christina followed Sir Owenday into the armory, sword in hand. She decided to come clean right away so he wouldn't be surprised by her lack of prowess.

"Sir Owenday, before we begin, I need to tell you something," she said in a tremulous voice.

"What's on your mind?" he asked kindly.

"I'm really bad at sports and things like that," she said quickly. "And I don't think I'll be any good at sword fighting. I just wanted you to know so you won't be shocked when you find out how terrible I am."

"Have you ever handled a sword before?"

She shook her head.

"Not to worry," the knight said soothingly. "We shall go slowly. But don't assume you won't be any good. Every great journey begins with a single step." After showing Christina how to grip her sword properly, he said, "Now let's see your swing."

She yelled and swung the sword as hard as she could. The weapon flew out of her hands, struck a rack of battle axes, and landed on the ground with a clatter.

Sir Owenday stroked his beard thoughtfully and said, "Not bad for a first-timer."

"Yeah, right," Christina muttered, convinced the knight was trying to spare her feelings.

Over the next three days, Christina practiced basic sword fighting techniques under Sir Owenday's patient instruction. To her dismay, she made no progress and found the whole affair to be tedious and demoralizing. This was exactly what she had feared, and it was all she could do to fight back the tears of frustration that assaulted her eyes.

Finally, during a particularly humiliating lesson on the fourth day, she flung her sword to the ground in anger. After shouting a series of words best left unwritten, she yelled, "That's it! I quit! I told you I'd be bad at this, didn't I? I'll never be a great warrior! Boriandar was crazy to choose me! Maybe I won't make a good queen after all! Maybe I'm just not good at anything!"

Christina stormed out of the armory and down the passageway. Belatro passed her, but she ignored his greeting. Once back in her bedchamber, she slammed the door shut and threw herself on her bed. After spending the next few minutes feeling sorry for herself, she heard a knock at the door. Sir Owenday. It had to be. Groaning, she sat up.

"Who is it?" she called out.

"May I come in, Christina?" It was Belatro.

"I guess," she sighed.

Upon entering, the jester somersaulted to the bed, flopped down on the edge of it, and looked at her.

"What do you want?" Christina asked grumpily.

"I'm sorry to disturb you," Belatro replied, "But you seemed upset, and I was wondering if there was something I could do to alleviate your troubles. Perhaps I can tell you a few jokes. I know a particularly funny one about an ogre and his gigantic –"

"No thank you, Bela," she interrupted. "I don't feel like laughing right now. And there's nothing you can do to help me, not unless you can turn me into a great sword fighter."

"Why would you want that?" Belatro asked. "You don't have to do any fighting at the Amber Castle. And when you drink the Elixir, you'll wield absolute power."

Christina sighed. "I don't know. I just thought it'd be neat if I turned out to be a talented sword fighter like the heroes in great tales."

"Well, you certainly don't need to wield a blade to be a hero."

"No, but I'm sure it helps."

Belatro sat down next to her. "Christina, there's a better way to win a fight. I like to say that a sharp mind can be deadlier than a sharp sword. In fact, I believe it's the greatest weapon of all. Any fool can wave a sword around."

"I don't believe that," she retorted. "You can't defeat villains with your mind."

"I beg to differ," Belatro replied indignantly. "I've often obtained the upper hand against more powerful foes with nothing more than my wits. And I'll wager you could, too."

Christina was about to make a snide remark to this when she heard footsteps approaching. A moment later, Sir Owenday and Gilfoit entered the room. As she stared at her two visitors, a wave of shame swept over Christina. She was about to apologize when Sir Owenday spoke.

"Christina, please accept my apology," he said.

She blinked. *"What?"*

"I believe I may have pushed you too hard," the knight said. "Perhaps you weren't ready for all of the things I tried to teach you. For that I'm sorry."

"No, I'm the one who should apologize," she said. "You weren't pushing that hard. You're a wonderful teacher. I just gave up too easily. I shouldn't have blown up at you. I'm really sorry, and I promise not to do that again. I'll be the perfect student from now on."

"Listen, Christina," Sir Owenday said. "If you don't want to continue the lessons, you don't have to. It's really not necessary that you learn how to use a sword or any other weapon."

"No, I want to give it another try," she said. "But just don't expect me to be good at it, okay?"

A grin spread over Sir Owenday's face. "Marvelous!" he said. "Not everyone is meant to be a great sword prodigy, but if you try your best, that shall be good enough for me."

"I wouldn't worry about your fighting skills, or lack thereof, Christina," Gilfoit said. "From what Sir Owenday has told me, you're far from being the worst sword fighter to emerge from the Well."

"Really?" she asked, amazed.

"Oh, yes," he replied. "Loads of children from the World Below were worse than you."

This cheered her up. "Thanks, Gil," she said, rising from the bed. "Sir Owenday, let's go back to the armory and continue my lesson." She turned to Belatro. "Thanks for visiting me, Bela. And I'm sorry I was cranky with you. You're probably right about the mind thing."

The jester smiled. "Think nothing of it, child. And always remember that sharp wits will help you when all other forms of aid have disappeared."

CHAPTER EIGHTEEN
BETWEEN REALITY AND DREAMS

By the end of Christina's first week in the Sanctuary, life had settled into a routine. She spent her mornings and afternoons training with Sir Owenday and even managed, to her great surprise, to make some progress. During the evenings, she sat in the library and pored over books on Imarian history or talked with her friends. Members of the Order were always coming in and out of the Sanctuary, and she was rarely given an opportunity to talk to any of them aside from Gilfoit, who had become a close companion. Whenever she encountered the other Order members, they were polite but formal, and she could never tell what they were thinking. This made her feel uneasy around them.

***

One day, after Christina had spent a fortnight in the Sanctuary, she was in the library reading about the military campaigns of Haroldine the Great when Lord Evermore summoned the future queen and her friends to the main hall. When they were all seated around a massive, round marble table that reminded Christina of the one King Arthur had at Camelot, the Head of the Order spoke.

"The entire kingdom has fallen and most of King James's soldiers have joined the rebels," he said. "He has fled to the Amber Castle with his few remaining supporters. The time has come for us to visit all of the regions of Imar and raise an army."

"When do we go?" Christina asked excitedly.

Lord Evermore smiled at her. "We'll leave at dawn the day after tomorrow. A few hours ago, I flew up to Ivenara and spoke with Hymral, leader of the rebels there, and she has agreed to accompany us with her celestonir army. And other Imarians will soon join our ranks. Thousands of rebels have already journeyed to the Eminent Dominion and surrounded the castle. We'll cross the mountains before traveling to the other lands, except for the Kaldewonn, of course."

"Why aren't we going there?" Christina asked. "Where is it? What's it like?"

"The Kaldewonn is a dark enchanted forest that lies directly south of the Well Plain," Gilfoit replied. "Everything I know about it is what I've heard in legends. It's supposed to be filled with wicked trees and creatures ruled by a powerful enchantress. Folks say she wears black armor and rides a man-eating horse. Fortunately, all of the creatures stay in the forest, and Imarians from other areas have the sense not to enter the place. Even the rulers never go there."

"Gilfoit is right," Lord Evermore said. "It's not a land we need to concern ourselves with. When we've built up our army, we'll march into the Eminent Dominion and put an end to King James's reign.

Christina, I told Hymral that you desired an empyremare, and she says you may have one as early as tomorrow. Would you like me to take you up to Ivenara in the morning?"

"Oh yes!" she cried. This news delighted her to no end. Back in her own world, she couldn't go to her favorite horse ranch, but here in this magical kingdom, she would get a unicorn that could actually fly!

Lord Evermore smiled. "Then it shall be done."

Later that night, as Christina lay in her bed, she resolved to stay in the kingdom after King James's death. She had been coming to this decision during the course of her quest, and it was clinched by the growing belief that it was her destiny to be the Eternal Ruler. The knowledge that she would receive her very own empyremare served to reinforce her intentions. Of course, she would miss her parents—even Mom—but, Christina told herself, the Imarians needed her to be their ruler and preserve the kingdom. Besides, Mom wouldn't miss her. Not after all the fights. And Dad obviously didn't miss Christina; he couldn't even be bothered to contact her after the divorce. And the kids at school would be glad she was gone, especially Sylvia.

***

When morning arrived, Lord Evermore and Christina mounted Taris and flew out of the Sanctuary and into the cool air. After soaring through a series of multicolored cloud ribbons, they entered a realm of green and yellow sky.

"We are now in the celestial country of Ivenara," Lord Evermore said to Christina, who sat in front of him.

"Wow!" she said, gazing upon glittering palaces with spiral towers that rested atop clear disks floating directly above gigantic silver cloud clusters. Sky nymphs—their naked snow-white bodies glistening with morning dew—stood on small clouds and watched the visitors with curiosity.

The Head of the Order steered his griffin toward a white palace, and Christina noticed a crowd of celestonirs milling about in front of a tall arched entryway. To her, they resembled human-sized fairies with sky-blue skin and giant butterfly wings. All of them wore cloaks of different colors. When Taris landed, the celestonirs cleared a path to the door.

"I've brought the child!" Lord Evermore cried. "This is Christina of the World Below!"

The celestonirs responded with bows. One of them shouted, "Long live the queen!" Others took up the cry and chanted their devotion to the new monarch. Once again, Christina's heart swelled, and she already felt like a great queen. After a moment, a celestonir approached the visitors. Christina couldn't help gazing admiringly at the creature's golden hair, which streamed down her back, and her black cloak covered with pictures of tiny silver moons.

"Welcome, Christina," she said with a heavenly smile. "I am Hymral, leader of the rebels. I understand that you desire an empyremare."

"Yes, please," Christina replied in a shy voice.

"Then I shall take you to the Glorious Pastures of the Oranbeorosphere to pick one out," Hymral said. "But first we would like to have a feast in your honor, if such is to your fancy."

"That would be great," Christina said. She couldn't wait to get her empyremare and wasn't really hungry but didn't want to hurt the feelings of her kind host.

Hymral smiled and helped her to the ground. Lord Evermore dismounted and the celestonir led her two guests into the palace with the others following closely behind. When Christina entered, she saw corridors leading in different directions. To her surprise, the place seemed barren—no personal touches to give it a homely aura. Apparently, the celestonirs preferred a monastic existence.

"To reach the dining hall, we must take a right at the end of this corridor," Hymral said. But Christina noticed that the corridor they were walking down was straight, and she could see no others that branched off from it. As they reached the end, the corridor suddenly bent to the right, and a new one appeared. At the end of this stood another arched entrance. She was surprised to see no doors in this palace and asked Hymral about it.

"We don't believe in shutting others out," the celestonir replied.

When Christina passed through the entrance, she found herself in a large room with a long sapphire table and chairs in the center. Ornate murals covered the walls, and Hymral told her that they depicted famous ancestors of the celestonirs. Christina sat at the head of the table, with Lord Evermore on her right and Hymral on her left. When everyone else had been seated, a column of servants arrived bearing white oval dishes covered with domed lids. As they set the dishes down and removed the lids, Christina saw what looked like clusters of little clouds. A servant scooped some of the strange food in his hand and put it on her plate. The other dinner guests helped themselves and used their fingers to eat. She did the same and discovered that the food tasted like a creamy, foamy cake; it was delicious. During the meal, the celestonirs drifted into conversation with one another, and Christina told Hymral about her adventures in the kingdom. When she finished, the celestonir said, "You're a very brave girl. It must have taken a great deal of courage to leave your world and come here."

"Not really," Christina replied. "I didn't like my life in Grand Rapids, and I hated living with my mom. I guess I just wanted to get away."

"Was your mother cruel to you?" Hymral asked, a concerned look on her face.

"Well—," Christina paused. She recalled how Mom had slapped her on the night she ran away from home but then found herself thinking about the horrible things she had said. The girl shifted uncomfortably in her chair before finishing her reply. "Not exactly. We just didn't get along."

Hymral nodded. "I see. Where was your father? Is he deceased?"

"No, he's still alive. My parents got divorced over a year ago, and my Dad moved to another state. I never see him anymore."

"So your mother looked after you all by herself. She must love you a great deal."

"Oh, she doesn't really care about me," Christina mumbled quickly. But for some reason, she realized that she didn't entirely believe this anymore. The conversation was causing her to feel terrible, so she changed the subject. "What's the Oranbeorosphere like?"

"It's the most beautiful place in this world," Hymral replied, giving Christina a discerning look. "We celestonirs call the Oranbeorosphere the meeting point between reality and dreams. In a short while, you shall see why."

***

When the feast ended, Christina and Lord Evermore mounted Taris and followed Hymral, who flapped her wings so rapidly that they were a blur. They flew high above the city before reaching an immense spiral cone of golden cloud chains. As they approached the summit, it became so bright that Christina had to shut her eyes. After a few moments, she felt gentle hands lifting her off the griffin and setting her down on something that felt like heavy air.

"Here we are, Christina," Hymral said in her lyrical voice. "Welcome to the Oranbeorosphere."

Christina cautiously opened her eyes and found herself standing upon an endless field of golden clouds. The sky here was a kaleidoscopic array of colors with thousands of twinkling white stars, giving her the impression that she was staring into a cosmic field of sparkling gemstones.

Hymral put her fingers in her mouth and let out a long whistle that sounded like a bird's song. Moments later, a celestonir holding a white staff flew over with a herd of empyremares. These celestial beasts had pure white skin, golden manes, and spiral horns, but Christina was surprised to discover that none of them had wings.

"Child, this is Morvandaer," Hymral said, motioning to the celestonir with the staff. "He's one of the best herders in Ivenara. Morvandaer, this is Christina of the World Below. She's to be our new queen."

Morvandaer came up to her and bowed. "It is an honor to meet you, Christina."

"Thank you," she replied. "Hymral said I might get my own empyremare today."

He nodded and uttered strange words to the empyremares. In response, the entire herd bowed before Christina.

"I've told them who you are, and they all desire to be yours," Morvandaer said, smiling. "Pick the one you want."

Christina surveyed the empyremares until a small one with a green star on its forehead caught her eye.

"There," she said, pointing at the animal. "Is it male or female?"

"Female," Morvandaer replied. He turned to call to the empyremare, but she trotted over to Christina and nuzzled her face as though she understood everything the girl had said.

"What's her name?"

"Alorynin. And you can't bestow another name upon her, for an empyremare will only answer to the one it was given at birth."

"That's alright. I think Alorynin's a great name." Christina looked at her new empyremare with affection. "I'll call you 'Ali' for short."

Ali nodded her head.

"How long do empyremares live for?" Christina asked.

"Actually, they never die of old age," Morvandaer replied.

"Really?"

Morvandaer nodded. "She'll be yours for as long as you live."

A thrill ran down Christina's spine. Since she was probably going to be the Eternal Ruler, she could keep Ali forever!

"Can I fly her around the Oranbeorosphere?" she asked, an eager look on her face.

The herder shook his head. "You must leave this place at once."

"Why? It's beautiful up here. Is there something dangerous about it?"

"The very beauty of the Oranbeorosphere is what makes it dangerous to those who aren't celestonirs," Hymral replied. "The longer you stay, the less you desire to return to the normal world. We usually don't allow outsiders to come here. However, since you're to be the new ruler, we made an exception. But you must go now."

"Alright," she said reluctantly.

"Child, do you want me to help you climb onto Ali's back?" Hymral asked.

"No, I can do it," Christina replied as she mounted her empyremare. The animal let out a joyful neigh.

"I think our new queen is going to be an expert rider," Lord Evermore said.

"I can see that," Morvandaer said with a smile. "Good luck, child. And may you have a fulfilling life."

"Thank you for the empyremare," Christina replied. "She's a dream come true."

***

After Christina and Lord Evermore flew back to the palace with Hymral, they said goodbye to their host and returned to the mountains. Christina loved soaring through the air on her empyremare; the experience gave her a feeling of complete freedom and happiness. When they reached the Sanctuary, Sir Owenday, Gilfoit, and the rest of the company met them. Everyone admired Ali, and Christina let them ride her empyremare for a while. When she had Ali all to herself again, she turned to Lord Evermore and asked, "If I stay in Imar and become the queen, can I ride her all day?"

He smiled. "As long it doesn't interfere with your royal duties. Remember, you'll still have a kingdom to rule."

CHAPTER NINETEEN
BELFYNOR

Early the next morning, Christina and her friends packed several chests with clothes, blankets, and other things for their journey through the kingdom. She shoved her old clothes and some of her new ones into her schoolbag, which she strapped on her back. Then everyone climbed on flying beasts and flew up one of the passageways and out of the Sanctuary.

Hymral and her celestonir warriors met the company outside, and everyone soared across the mountains. Christina felt glad to be leaving the confines of the Sanctuary and continuing with her quest, and she enjoyed watching the celestonirs in flight, with their diamond-shaped formations and flapping butterfly wings. To her, they resembled a heavenly host of angel warriors.

When evening fell, the army stopped in a wide valley to rest for the night. A cave with two crumbling statues of dwarf kings flanking either side of the entrance offered the only shelter in the area. After checking to make sure there were no unwelcome inhabitants inside, Lord Evermore told Christina that she and her friends might sleep there if they wished.

He and the other Order members—except for Gilfoit, who stayed with Christina—pitched their tents outside while celestonir guards watched over the encampment from above.

At the back of the cave, Gilfoit built a small fire while Christina and the rest of her friends made themselves comfortable. Eelweed leaned against the rock wall when it suddenly moved backward, revealing a narrow opening through which he fell.

"I'm coming, Eelweed!" Christina shouted as the water gnome's cries for help faded, and she leapt into the opening before anyone could stop her. She slid down a smooth, steep passage and collided with Eelweed, who was trying to crawl back up. The two of them tumbled to the hard earth at the bottom. Christina rose and saw that they were in a large cavern. Long stalactites hung from the ceiling, and a dim orange light came from a source she couldn't yet discern.

"Eelweed, are you alright?" she asked. He responded by pushing her back up the passage. "Hey, what's the problem?"

"Hurry!" he cried in a panicked voice. "It'll eat us alive!"

"What are you talking...?" Her voice trailed off as she looked over his shoulder. A huge dragon sat on a pile of stones not more than thirty feet in front of her. This great, fearsome-looking lizard had leathery gray flesh and bat-like wings, and short golden spikes protruded down the length of his spine and tail. Long talons jutted from his feet, and a pair of bulbous orange eyes peered through wide, narrow slits on the sides of his reptilian head. It was these eyes that provided the light in the cavern.

Shock prevented Christina from speaking, and it took her several seconds to regain her voice. When she did, she screamed. She and Eelweed tried to scramble up the slippery passage but kept sliding back down. Christina expected the two of them to be burnt to a crisp at any moment, but nothing happened. Suddenly, they were knocked backward by Sir Owenday, Gilfoit, and Belatro, who were descending down the passage. When Gilfoit saw the dragon, the normally stoic dwarf lost his composure and let out a high-pitched shriek. He, too, tried to crawl back up the tunnel but failed. Gilfoit, Belatro, and Eelweed crowded behind Sir Owenday and pushed him forward.

"Sir Knight, now's your chance to prove your worth!" Gilfoit said, his voice having regained its usual timbre. "If you slay this dragon, you'll be the most honored knight in the kingdom, horse or no horse!"

Sir Owenday gripped his sword and shield tightly, and the sound of his shaking body made Christina think of rattling aluminum cans. He pulled up the visor on his helmet so the dragon could see his face.

"Y-y-your d-days are n-n-n-numbered, f-fiend!" he stuttered.

Instead of attacking, the dragon merely stared at him, and Christina thought she saw an amused smile tug at the corners of his wide mouth.

"I've been waiting for a knight to come to my lair," the dragon said in a deep, guttural voice. "Of course, I had hoped for that day to arrive a few centuries sooner, but I suppose later is better than never." He rolled over on his side and pointed to a small dark patch on the lower part of his scaly underbelly. "Stab me right here with your blade, if you please. This is my weak spot. Yes, that should do the trick."

It would be difficult to say which member of the company was more shocked. For the next few moments, Sir Owenday didn't move or speak. He merely stood there with his mouth open and a blank expression on his face.

"Come again?" he spluttered after an interminable silence.

"I said you can kill me," the dragon replied.

"You mean you don't care if you die?"

"Not too bright, is he?" the dragon asked, grinning at Christina and showing rows of enormous yellow teeth. "I never suspected that humans could be *this* dim-witted."

"Why do you want to die, Mr. Dragon?" she asked, her fear now replaced by curiosity.

"Belfynor is my name," he replied. "I have lived my entire life in despair."

"What's wrong?" Belatro asked.

"Let me show you," Belfynor replied. The dragon rolled over on his stomach and raised his head. Facing his visitors, he took a deep breath and exhaled. Christina and her friends scattered in different directions in a desperate search for cover, but nothing emerged from Belfynor's mouth except several weak plumes of black smoke.

Christina, who had expected to be covered with third-degree burns, stared at Belfynor in amazement.

"You can't make fire?" she asked.

The dragon shook his great head. "I was born with a lung disorder that prevents me from emitting flames.

When I was a hatchling, my parents had a renowned warlock visit our lair. He informed them that a simple operation would fix this ailment, but this operation is very dangerous for the one performing it, and there's no guarantee of success. The warlock refused to help me because he was afraid of getting burnt. My father approached many other warlocks in the kingdom, but they all refused as well. So I was stuck with this condition."

"That's awful," Eelweed said, scratching his left gill.

Belfynor nodded. "The rest of the dragons treated me as an outcast. They wouldn't let me fly on raids with them or fight in battles. They mocked me and said I would never be any good. Now all of the other dragons in the kingdom have died or been slain, and I've become a recluse. I've always wanted to be fierce, but I lack a dragon's most important feature. I've long hoped that a knight would come and kill me and thus end my misery."

"I know what it's like to not be normal or popular," Christina said. "The other kids at my school back home didn't like me because I read books all the time and wasn't interested in clothes, makeup, and all that other stuff."

"I, too, know the misery that accompanies the outcast," Sir Owenday said. "Many years ago, a witch put a curse on me so I couldn't ride a horse. Now all of the other knights mock me." He lowered his sword. "I was raised to believe that dragons were foul creatures, but you seem like a decent fellow. I'm sorry, but I can't bring myself to harm you."

Christina thought quickly. "I have an idea, Belfy," she said. "I came up the Well of Rulers, and I'm the new queen of Imar—or will be when King James is dead. I'm gathering an army right now, and we're going to march on the Amber Castle. How would you like to join me? I know you can't breathe fire, but you could still do some serious damage."

The dragon's eyes lit up. "You're the monarch of our kingdom?" he asked excitedly.

"Yes. My name is Christina, and I want you to fight for me. And I'd like you to be our friend, if that's all right with you."

Belfynor mulled over this offer. "I've never had a friend before," he said after a spell. "But I've always wanted one. I'd like to join you, child, but I'm afraid that others will laugh at me when they discover my problem."

Christina shook her head. "You don't need to make fire to be fierce. If you joined me, you'd be the only dragon in our army. No one will laugh at you."

"Very well," Belfynor replied. "I'll do it."

"Thank you!" she said. "But I don't want you attacking innocent people. Just the bad ones."

"Not to worry," he replied. "You're the queen, so if you command it, I shall obey."

"Good," she said. "Now let me introduce you to my other friends. Belfy, this is Sir Owenday, Gilfoit, Eelweed, and Belatro."

"I'm very pleased to meet all of you," the dragon said. "And now that we're friends, let me give you a special dragon hug."

Before the others could reply, he snatched them up in his huge forearms and held them tightly to his scaly chest.

129

"Hey, let us go!" Gilfoit cried. Christina couldn't speak because her mouth was pressed against Belfynor's hide. The girl felt as though she was suffocating, and she thought she heard bones breaking. When the dragon finally released his new friends, she gasped for air.

"Please don't do that again," she panted.

"Yes, no more hugs from you," Sir Owenday said. "You bent my shield."

"How are we going to leave this cave?" Eelweed asked. "We have to reach our encampment. We can't crawl up this passage, and even if we could, Belfynor certainly wouldn't fit through there."

"Not to worry, my good water gnome," the dragon said. "There's a larger passage somewhere at the end of this cavern. Haven't used it in centuries, but it should still work. Follow me."

He led the others to the back of his lair, where they saw two large tunnels.

"Which one leads to the outside?" Gilfoit asked.

"I think it's the one on the right," Belfynor replied. "Yes, I'm certain of it. I may be a thousand years old, but we dragons have long memories. Now if the rest of you will get on, I'll fly us all out of here."

Belfynor lay on his stomach, and after his new friends climbed on his back and gripped the spikes, he raised himself up on all four legs and ran down the tunnel. When he had picked up enough speed, he flapped his wings and lifted off into the dark, musty air. As Belfynor approached the end of the tunnel, Christina realized, to her horror, that enormous gray boulders blocked the opening.

"We're going to crash!" Belatro screamed.

"Not to worry," Belfynor replied calmly. "With enough speed and power, I can smash my way through!"

"But those rocks will hit the rest of us!" Christina protested.

"I don't think so," the dragon said. "We'll be going so fast that none of them should touch you. Still," he added, looking back at her with a devilish grin, "I'd duck if I were you!"

As Belfynor picked up speed, Christina closed her eyes and bent her head down as low as she could. Soon there was a loud *thud!* When she opened her eyes, she saw the starry night sky. The open air chilled her pale skin, and she shivered.

"Where is this encampment of yours?" Belfynor asked, soaring to the top of the mountains.

"I'm not certain," Gilfoit said. "It's too dark to see."

"Oh, don't worry about that," Belfynor said. "I can see clearly in the dark. Tell me what to look for."

"We were staying in a valley that had a cave with two dwarf statues at the entrance," Christina replied. "There's a bunch of tents outside and an army of celestonirs hovering in the air. The celestonirs! I almost forgot! Gil, won't they shoot at Belfy when we get closer?"

"I hadn't thought of that," Gilfoit replied. "Belfynor, do you think you could see our encampment from afar?"

"Of course," the dragon replied. "In fact, I think I see it now."

"Very well," Gilfoit said. "Drop us off a good distance away so the celestonirs can't spot us. We'll walk over to the campsite, find Lord Evermore, and bring him over to see you. The last thing we need is to get shot at by a thousand arrows."

Belfynor landed near a clump of trees at the top of the valley. When Christina and her friends climbed off his back, they could see tiny dots of firelight far below.

"Thanks, Belfy," she said. "We'll be back in a short while."

"Could one of you stay here with me?" Belfynor asked. "It's been a long time since I had any company."

"I'll stay with you," Sir Owenday replied. "We can talk knight-to-dragon. I must say, I've enjoyed flying on your back. Since I can't ride a horse, would you mind serving as my means of travel?"

Belfynor bowed his head and held out his right forefoot in a grand gesture. "It would be my pleasure, Sir Knight."

The others made their way down the side of the valley and walked toward the campfires. When they were about a hundred feet away, Hymral and several celestonirs flew toward them.

"Where were you, Christina?" she asked. "We've been searching all over for you."

Christina told her what happened. When they reached the encampment, Lord Evermore met them.

"Thank Ethindir, you're alive!" he said, embracing her. "Your loss would have been a terrible blow to this kingdom. When I heard about the secret passage, I tried to send others after you, but the wall wouldn't open again. Where's Sir Owenday?"

"Oh, he's with the dragon," she replied, enjoying the look that this statement produced on Lord

Evermore's face. After Christina retold the story of what occurred in Belfynor's lair, she said, "Will you come with us to meet him? You'll find he's harmless. Then we can all come back here."

Lord Evermore agreed to this, so Christina and the others led him to the trees while Hymral and the celestonirs returned to their positions. As they walked, Christina asked, "Do you know what that secret passage was for?"

"That was a dwarf tunnel," Lord Evermore replied. "In the days before Haroldine the Great, the dwarfs fought constantly with the ogres and other mountain creatures that are now extinct. They built those secret passages as a means of escape in times of trouble. After you folks disappeared down that hole, I saw a tiny faded rune on the cave wall near the opening. When I checked the cave earlier, I hadn't noticed it, and for that I apologize. If anything had happened to you, Christina, it would have been my fault."

"That's okay," she said. "We got a dragon now, and he's going to help us take the Amber Castle."

When the group reached the tree grove, she introduced Belfynor to the Head of the Order.

"Pleased to meet you, Belfynor," Lord Evermore said. "I understand you're to aid us in the coming battle against King James."

"That's right."

"Then on behalf of the Order, I give you my thanks."

Belfynor's face flushed a deep purple. "Pray, don't mention it," he said with modesty.

"Now we had best return to the encampment and get some rest," Lord Evermore said. "We have much traveling to do tomorrow."

"I've promised Christina I wouldn't attack any good humans or creatures," Belfynor said, "But I hope there'll be plenty of enemies to destroy."

Lord Evermore nodded his head. "There will be, Belfynor. I promise you, there will be."

CHAPTER TWENTY
THE BATTLE OF THE AMBER CASTLE

On the following day, Christina and her army continued their journey through the kingdom, and before long, they were joined by thousands of Imarians. Since most of her soldiers didn't possess flying beasts, she and Ali traveled by ground, but Christina didn't mind this.

The future queen was treated with reverence wherever she went. However, Christina quickly realized that her popularity in this kingdom—which she previously enjoyed—now made her feel hollow inside. Although it *was* better to be the object of adulation rather than scorn, she knew these Imarians only loved her because she was the new ruler. Christina was fond of Gilfoit, Sir Owenday, and the other friends she had made during her quest but often wondered if they really liked her for who she was and not for the title she possessed.

When the army finally came to the Eminent Dominion, it passed through a series of towns and cities before entering a desert whose soft sand shone a brilliant emerald. As she and Ali crested a sand dune, Christina saw the Amber Castle for the first time. Situated on an island in the middle of an oval lake, the castle boasted several immense towers and a formidable curtain wall.

The army joined up with the rebels who surrounded the island, and Christina's total force swelled to fifty thousand combatants. The ground soldiers held positions around the lake while keeping far out of range of the enemy's catapults. The celestonirs and other soldiers on griffins hovered above the castle to make sure no one could leave undetected, and dwarf engineers built ladders, boats, and bridges for the upcoming invasion. Christina and the Order members set up their encampment on the side of the shore facing the castle entrance.

Later that evening, as Christina and her friends ate dinner in their tent, Lord Evermore walked in and said, "All of you should get a good night's rest. The army will attack at first light."

"Can't you just get some catapults and pulverize the castle to dust?" Christina asked.

He shook his head. "That castle was built by Ethindir. He put some powerful enchantments into the walls so they couldn't decay or be destroyed by any device of human or creature."

"Are there any secret passageways into the castle?" Eelweed asked.

"No," Gilfoit replied. "And even if there were, they would have been sealed up ages ago."

"Do you know how many soldiers the king has?" Sir Owenday asked.

"Some of the local people informed me that he has around a thousand followers with him," Lord Evermore replied. "And most of them are inside the castle. Sir Owenday, would you like to join the attack?"

"Yes, but I've sworn an oath to protect Christina," the knight replied.

"The child will be quite safe," Lord Evermore assured him. "We'll be with her."

"Go ahead and join the battle, Sir Owenday," Christina said. "I'll be fine."

"Very well," Sir Owenday replied. "Then I shall fight with your army."

"Good," Lord Evermore said, and departed. The others finished their meal and went straight to bed, for they were all very tired after the long journey.

**

An hour later, everyone was awakened by a distant cacophony of sounds. Christina heard screams and the clanking of weapons coming from the island. The tent flap opened, and Albrik stepped inside.

"What's happening out there?" Gilfoit asked.

"The king's men killed some of our celestonirs with arrows and fired catapults at the soldiers on the northern shore," Albrik replied. "The rest of the celestonirs responded by attacking the Amber Castle, and now the others are taking boats to the island to join them. The battle is on! I've come to fetch Sir Owenday. Belfynor is waiting outside. He'll fly you to the island."

"What about the Ifarthians?" Christina asked.

"The miniatures?" Belatro replied. "What about them?"

"They haven't arrived yet," she said. "I promised them they could participate in the battle."

Albrik gave a dismissive wave of his hand. "Forget about those tiny people. If they can't come on time, that's their fault. And besides, they'd be no use in battle anyhow."

Not wanting to argue, Christina made no reply to this. She followed the others out of the tent, and after Sir Owenday and Belfynor flew off toward the castle, Albrik said, "Let's go watch the battle! Come on, everyone!"

So they all clambered up a steep, high sand dune. Although the sun had set, the cloudless, pale lilac sky of early twilight provided plenty of light to see with. Fascinated, Christina watched the battle taking place less than a thousand yards away, the participants resembling tiny figures to her.

Legions of celestonirs and other warriors on griffins and perytons loosed volleys of arrows at the king's soldiers situated on the castle grounds, in towers, and along the top of the curtain wall. The defenders outside of the castle responded with bows and catapults while their comrades inside shot arrows through windows and slits. Meanwhile, humans, dwarfs, polevicks, and other creatures on small makeshift boats paddled furiously toward the island, but they were soon overtaken by water gnomes and ogres, who didn't require watercraft to get across the lake. Christina saw many of her soldiers fall in battle, their dying screams echoing in her mind. She felt sick but couldn't help watching the carnage unfolding before her eyes.

Christina soon heard a dragon's roar that made the sand around her feet quake slightly. By this time, the king soldiers outside were giving way to the attackers, and when they saw Belfynor flying toward them with bared teeth, they screamed and ran for the high arched doors that served as the castle's main entrance. When the last surviving defender was safely inside, the doors were closed and bolted. The first ogre to reach the island scaled the curtain wall and opened a portcullis flanked between two towers. Within minutes, thousands of Christina's soldiers poured on to the castle grounds.

"We may as well go back down," Gilfoit said. "They'll bring a battering ram to breach the main doors, but we won't be able to see what's going on inside the castle."

Christina felt a wave of relief as she turned away from the battle. When the group returned to their campsite, Gilfoit, Eelweed, and Belatro sat around a fire to discuss the events taking place a short distance away. Christina returned to the tent on the pretext that she was exhausted and wanted to go back to sleep; in truth, she wanted to be alone. Although her quest was nearly over, she felt anything but happy. Something was wrong, but she didn't know what. After a restless hour, she decided to go outside and get some fresh air. But when she approached the tent flap, she heard her friends talking about her.

"She would never do anything so terrible," Belatro said. "I refuse to believe it."

"But if she isn't the subject of the Prophecy, she'll turn out like King James and the others," Gilfoit said. "Many children have come up the Well, but there's only one Eternal Ruler. The chance Christina will be that person is slim."

"But we have waited for eight thousand years," Eelweed said. "Certainly the time has come."

"I bet Christina's the One," Belatro said. "I've taken a real liking to her."

"Christina seems a good person," Gilfoit said. "But if she goes the way of the other rulers, the Cycle will continue, and it has allowed Imar to remain the greatest kingdom in Myredan. And there's another thing to keep in mind here. All of the children who came to Imar did so because they led a miserable existence in their own world. The Elixir of Purity and the Sword of Etossar allowed them to live in royal splendor and wield enormous power for centuries."

"That may be," Belatro replied. "But it tears me up inside to know what ultimately happens to them. What a tragedy it is to gain an entire kingdom but lose one's soul in the end! I don't care what anyone says. It's a terrible price to pay."

"Gilfoit, you were there when the other kings and queens took the throne," Eelweed said. "What were they like in the beginning?"

"Wonderful," he replied. "I remember King James in particular. He was called Jim in the World Below and was the kindest person one could meet. When the king first arrived in Imar, he told me that in his own world, the other children mocked him because he was different. That was one of the reasons why he accepted the quest. The same is true for the other children who came here. I agree it's terrible what the Elixir does to these humans, but they made their choice. That's how the Cycle works. I've seen this process repeat itself many, many times."

"At least there's a bright spot for the rest of us," Belatro said. "If Christina doesn't turn out to be the One, we'll be long departed from this life before she becomes corrupt and wicked. At least we'll die remembering her as she is now."

Christina couldn't listen to any more of this, so she crept back to bed. Shocked and disheartened to learn that she wasn't the only child who had felt like an outcast in the World Below, she lay on her blanket as doubt flooded her mind. At that moment, Christina could no longer imagine being the Eternal Ruler. Instead, she saw herself as a sad and confused girl in a place where she didn't belong. She had often felt this way back in Grand Rapids, but here in this strange faraway kingdom, the feeling was ten times worse.

She wondered if her predecessors had experienced similar emotions during their quests. Surely, they had all believed they would turn out to be the Eternal Ruler. Or had they? Back in Ferncandell Forest, Gilfoit told her that dozens of children came to the kingdom, and all of them decided to stay and take the throne, but the more Christina considered this, the less plausible it seemed. There must have been at least *some* children who had decided not to drink the Elixir. But if *that* was true, then why didn't they go home?

A terrible thought entered Christina's mind, and she checked it immediately. But her determination to stay in the kingdom waned, and she felt even more terrible than she had after leaving home and realizing there was no clear path out of her predicament.

CHAPTER TWENTY-ONE
REVELATION

Christina was awakened the next morning by Ali's thick, warm tongue caressing her cheek. Sitting up, she saw that the tent was empty. After stroking her empyremare's mane for a few minutes, Christina led her outside, where Gilfoit, Eelweed, and Belatro were waiting for her. The others were still away, and there was a frenzy of activity around the encampment. Soldiers were pulling up tents, packing belongings, and departing for their homes.

"Good morning, Christina," Gilfoit said, scratching his beard lazily. "How are you feeling today?"

"I've got a headache."

"Are you ready to fulfill your destiny and become our new queen?"

Christina didn't know how to respond, so she changed the subject. "Is the battle over?"

Gilfoit nodded. "Your soldiers took it hours ago. Most of them have already left."

"How'd everything go? How many did we lose?"

"Our side lost over a thousand warriors," Gilfoit said in a somber voice. "But the outcome was never in doubt, and every one of the king's soldiers died fighting for their ruler."

"Where's Belfy and Sir Owenday?" she asked. "Are they alright?"

"The dragon and the knight are fine," Gilfoit replied. "They're at the castle."

"What about King James? Did he fight in the battle?"

Gilfoit gave a contemptuous laugh. "He was nowhere to be seen. That rat is holed up in the Throne Room, as we knew he would be. But some of your ogres found his empyremare and ate her."

Christina was horrified. "That's awful!" she said. "The poor thing did nothing wrong! How could you let that happen?"

Gilfoit shrugged. "Why should I have stopped them? Those ogres were mighty hungry after doing all that fighting. I've come to take you to the castle. The Throne Room has front and back doors, and they can only be opened from the outside by a child from the World Below. Lord Evermore and the other members of the Order are waiting at the entrance. Are you ready?"

Though she grappled internally with conflicting thoughts and emotions, a surge of desire to be the Eternal Ruler and enjoy her empyremare ran through Christina's mind, and she took a deep breath and said, "Let's go. Can Eelweed and Belatro come with us?"

"They may come into the castle but not the Throne Room," Gilfoit replied. "Not until the succession is complete. It's a sacred tradition of ours. But don't worry; we shan't be in there long. Leave your empyremare. She'll be fine."

Christina assented to this, but she felt uneasy. Gilfoit wasn't his usual friendly self; his tone was stiff and formal. She kissed Ali on the nose and told her she would be back in a few minutes. The empyremare nodded and stood rooted to the spot as if to say *I'll be right here.* When the company reached the edge of the encampment, they heard a voice cry out, "Your Majesty!"

Everyone turned around and saw a miniature riding toward them on a glass horse.

"Sir Kranwick!" Christina said delightedly.

"Greetings!" he replied, and gestured toward a sand dune in the distance. "The Ifarthians are behind that hill! We've made it at last! When's the battle? Are there any boats available to take all of us to the castle?"

"Unfortunately, Sir Knight, the battle is over," Gilfoit said, a bemused look on his face.

"I'm sorry, Sir Kranwick," Christina said. "The army planned to invade the castle this morning, but the battle started last night after some of our soldiers were killed."

For several tense moments, the miniature knight made no reply. Then he said, "I can be chivalric about this, though my heart aches grievously. If my countrymen and I can't be of any assistance, then there's nothing left for us to do but return to our land."

With head bowed, he turned his horse around and headed in the direction from which he came.

***

Gilfoit led the others down to the lake, where a human took them all to the island in a small boat. When they reached the curtain wall, an ogre opened the portcullis for them. Upon entering the castle grounds, Christina beheld sprawling flower gardens dotted with marble statues of various nymphs, but the corpses of dead soldiers defiled this otherwise magnificent scenery. The results of the previous night's carnage nauseated her. Hearing someone shout her name from above, she looked up and saw Sir Owenday astride Belfynor, who was perched on top of a tower. They waved at her, and she gave a half-hearted wave in response.

When the company reached the front of the Amber Castle, another ogre opened the main doors leading inside. Gilfoit took Christina and the others down a long, wide hall lined with doors, staircases, and towering pillars bearing the royal coat of arms. Another set of double doors with golden handles shaped like ouroboros's formed a high arch at the far end of the hall. Lord Evermore and the rest of the Order stood in front of the doors.

"Welcome, Christina," he said. "Your time has come. You must grab both doorknobs simultaneously to open the doors. When this is done, we shall go in first. Follow us and close the doors behind you."

After she grasped the knobs, which began to glow, she pulled the doors outward and looked inside the Throne Room. The walls were lined with ornate tapestries featuring past rulers of the kingdom, and a road of thick violet carpet ran from the doors to the oval dais where the throne sat. The little diamond table she had seen in the forest stood next to the throne. But no flask rested upon it, nor was anyone sitting on the throne. King James was nowhere to be seen.

"Where is he?" Christina asked in surprise.

"He's in here somewhere," Lord Evermore replied. He swiftly entered the Throne Room, and the other Order members followed.

"Do you want us to come in with you, Christina?" Eelweed asked. "I don't care what the rules are. We'll remain with you if that's what you wish."

"I think I'll be alright," she replied in a voice that masked her anxiety. "This won't take long. I'll be back in a few minutes."

Reluctantly, she walked into the Throne Room and closed the doors behind her.

The Order's search didn't take long, for the room contained few hiding places. Gilfoit and Albrik looked behind the throne and pulled out a shrieking, disheveled King James. He dropped the flask, and his crown fell to the floor. A human Order member named Krannock quickly scooped them up.

"Christina," Lord Evermore said, "The monster who killed your friend and tried to do the same to you is at your mercy. Now you can wreak your vengeance upon this miserable toad."

"Oh no!" she replied. "I don't want to be the one to kill him!"

Lord Evermore nodded and said, "Very well."

And without another word, he thrust his sword into the king's heart. Gilfoit and Albrik let go of him, and he collapsed on the floor and writhed in agony. Horrified, Christina looked away. The king's execution sickened her as much as Eorin's had. Although Eorin had been her friend and rescuer while King James had been a tyrant, the latter was, after all, once an innocent child from the World Below.

As soon as the king was dead, the Elixir's color turned from black to a milky white, and Krannock handed the flask and crown over to Lord Evermore, who took them and walked up to Christina.

"Congratulations, Your Majesty," he said, placing the crown on her head. "You are now Queen Christina of Imar."

He bowed low, and so did the other Order members. When Lord Evermore raised his head, he held out the flask. She took it and stared at the Elixir.

"Your Majesty, I don't mean to rush you, but you must drink it immediately," he said. "We can't waste any more time. Once the Elixir is in your body, the succession will be complete."

Feeling as though a gigantic boulder was pressing down on her, Christina slowly removed the stopper, and a geyser of Elixir shot into the air. She brought the flask to her lips but went no further. The part of her that wanted to remain in the kingdom made one last effort to conjure up her waning hatred of her mother and her life in the World Below.

The fights with Mom raced through her mind, but she now reflected upon her own words and actions with sharp clarity. The unhappiness and anger that drove Christina to leave home was gone, and instead of seeing herself as an innocent child who had been wronged, she now saw a selfish and spiteful person, and she knew she could no longer blame Mom for everything bad in her life. Then Christina recalled how Mom had attempted to connect with her, only to be brushed off with disdain; yet, as Hymral had observed, Mom stayed with her after Dad left. The realization that her mother loved her and that she loved her mother hit the queen like a thunderbolt. A tidal wave of homesickness engulfed her, and she lowered the flask.

"Is something wrong, Your Majesty?" Gilfoit asked in alarm.

"Yes," she replied, laying crown, sword, and flask on the floor by her feet. "I don't want to be your queen. I want to go home to my mother. I'm sorry about this."

"You have nothing to apologize for," Lord Evermore said, picking up the objects. "But I do, for I'm afraid I can't allow you to leave this kingdom."

"What are you talking about?" she asked. A feeling of terror seized her as she recalled the terrible thought she had briefly entertained the night before.

"Your inability to rule leaves me no choice but to assume the role of Steward of the Kingdom," he replied. "You are clearly distraught as a result of your quest. That is the only logical explanation I can find for your erratic behavior. You are not yourself. Indeed, I believe you are mad. No sane human or creature would refuse immortality and absolute power. You only need to rest a bit and think things over."

"No, I don't!" she shouted. "I've made up my mind! Ethindir gave me a choice!"

But Lord Evermore paid no attention to her. "Gilfoit, take her out through the back and lock her in the Tower of Mendomir," he said. "I want you to stand guard at the door. Your Majesty, I shall see you in twelve hours, and, hopefully, you'll have had a change of heart by then. Until that time, we shall take care of your empyremare, and you may have her back when you're ready to fulfill your destiny. But if you continue to remain obstinate in your folly, we shall have no choice but to compel you to drink the Elixir."

"But you can't make me drink that stuff!" she replied. "I know how it works! If you try, it'll just run down the front of my body!"

Lord Evermore nodded. "That's true. We can't *force* the Elixir down your throat. But you *will* drink it of your own accord, even if we have to employ certain means to persuade you. We have much experience in this particular matter. After all, you're not the first child to hesitate before taking the throne."

Christina rounded on Gilfoit, a hurt look on her face. "You lied to me," she said, and her insides felt like ice. "You told me that no child from the World Below chose to go home."

"I assure you, Your Majesty, he spoke the truth," Lord Evermore said. "In the end, all of the children chose to stay, even if a number of them needed our help to make that decision. But believe me, once you swallow the Elixir, you'll realize you made the right choice, as did your predecessors."

As the meaning of these words sank in, Gilfoit walked over to Christina and grabbed her by the arm.

"Let go of me!" she cried, trying to break loose.

"I'm sorry, Your Majesty," he said, and there was a strange detachment in his voice. "This is for your own good as well as the kingdom's."

"I'm your queen!" she said. "I'm *ordering* you to release me!"

"But you're no longer the one with the power," he replied. "Not until you drink the Elixir."

"I thought we were friends," she said in a pained voice.

"My friends are in the Order," he replied coldly. "You're merely another child for me to put on the throne."

These last words stung Christina's heart. She screamed and struggled to free herself, but Gilfoit held her firmly as he dragged her from the Throne Room.

CHAPTER TWENTY-TWO
THE PRISONER IN THE TOWER

When Gilfoit reached the Tower of Mendomir with his prisoner, he pulled open the door and pushed her inside. Christina hit the smooth amber floor with a loud *smack!* She rose quickly and ran to the door, but her captor had already shut and locked it. She banged her fists as hard as she could against the heavy oak and screamed to be let out; her pleas went ignored. After several minutes of this, she gave up.

Christina turned around and saw that the square tower was immaculate, not dirty or cobweb-ridden like the ones she read about in stories. The room was empty and spacious. There were no windows, but in one of the corners, a steep staircase led up to a small door. Hoping to find a way to escape, she ran up the stairs, opened the door, and walked out on to a small balcony with a parapet running along the edge. Looking down, she saw, to her great disappointment, that she was several hundred feet from the ground with no way to reach it.

Christina could see part of the island far below her. Humans and creatures moved about, and they looked like ants to her. She screamed for help, but no one seemed to hear. Raising her head, she spotted two men sitting on griffins several feet above her; each of them wore a silver cloak and held a bow. Order members. Lord Evermore probably put them there to guard her. The men didn't acknowledge her presence but kept a watchful vigil. Christina returned to the bottom of the tower, lay on the floor, and cried herself to sleep.

***

Several hours later, she awakened to the sound of someone whispering her name. Thinking that her captors had come back for her, she glanced at the door. But it remained shut, and she quickly realized that the sound came from above. Looking up, Christina saw Sir Owenday and Belatro standing at the top of the stairs. She ran up to her two friends and gave them a hug.

"How did you get here?" she asked.

The knight put a finger to his lips. "Quiet, Your Majesty. Noise carries far in this castle. You left this in the tent." He handed Christina her schoolbag.

"Thanks," she said in a softer voice before repeating her question.

Sir Owenday opened the door, and she saw Belfynor hovering right above the railing with Eelweed on his back. The knight closed the door again.

"The rest of us grew worried when you didn't emerge from the Throne Room," Belatro said. "We went to Lord Evermore, and he told us that you rejected the crown, the flask, and the Sword. He also claimed to be Steward of Imar and said you would be released from this tower when you 'came to your senses.' He allowed us to see you on the condition that we attempt to use our friendship to persuade you to drink the Elixir."

"I don't want to stay here," Christina said, backing away. Sir Owenday and Belatro no longer seemed like saviors, but potential betrayers. "I want to go home."

"But I thought you hated your life in the World Below and that you desired to be our queen," Sir Owenday said.

"I was wrong," she replied, "About that and a lot of other things. I was wrong about my mom. I was wrong about my dad. And I was wrong about *me*. I'm not the Eternal Ruler, and to tell you the truth, I don't want to be. The last thing I told my mom before I ran away was that I hated her. But I don't. I love her, and I want to go home and make things right."

Sir Owenday nodded. "Then we'll have to resort to our alternate plan. Right before we came here, we talked it over and agreed that if we couldn't persuade you to drink the Elixir, we would take you to the Well. Gilfoit told us that the Order was going to fetch you tonight to compel you to complete the succession, so we decided to reach you first. I don't quite understand everything that is going on, and Gilfoit wouldn't elaborate, but something seems terribly wrong here."

"Lord Evermore said he and the Order were going to torture me if I still refused to drink the Elixir, even though Ethindir gave me the choice to stay or leave," Christina replied. "They've been doing this with other children from my world. That's why the Well has never been destroyed."

"Then we'd best depart right away," Belatro said.

"But why would you want to help me?" Christina asked, suspecting a trap.

"You're our queen now, Your Majesty," Sir Owenday replied. "And if you wish to go home, then it's our duty to help you get there, even at the risk of our own lives."

Although her suspicions disappeared, Christina was disappointed to learn that her friends were only helping her because she was the queen. Still, she was desperate to get home and wasn't about to carp over the motives of anyone willing to give her aid.

"Your Majesty, did you really think we would abandon you in your hour of need?" Belatro asked.

"Gil did," she muttered.

"He feels that his loyalty to the Order is more important than his loyalty to his queen," Sir Owenday replied. "And he doubtless believes in the Prophecy."

"But don't you two believe in the Prophecy?" Christina asked.

"I don't know if the Prophecy is genuine or not," Belatro replied with a shrug.

"Not all prophecies come true," Sir Owenday added. "I suppose we'll soon see about this one."

"Wait!" Christina said to him. "Lord Evermore has the flask and the Sword, and I need those to destroy the Well and go home!"

"Are you certain he still possesses them, Your Majesty?" Belatro replied in a sly voice. She turned to face the jester and saw that he held the two objects in his hands.

"How did you get them?" she asked in surprise.

"I filched these from Lord Evermore," he said. "Thought they might come in handy. Did I not tell you I was a great pickpocket? You saved me in the forest, so it was the least I could do. But we had better hurry. He will soon discover their absence."

Suddenly, they heard a cry of shock and anger from somewhere in the castle.

"On second thought, make that right now," Belatro said.

"Quick!" Sir Owenday said.

Christina took the Sword and flask and kissed Sir Owenday and Belatro on the cheek before following them onto the balcony.

"Are we taking her home?" Belfynor asked, flying in circles.

"Yes!" she shouted up to him. "Let's get out of here!"

The guards, who had been keeping close watch on Belfynor, prepared to shoot arrows at him, but the dragon knocked the two of them off their griffins with a powerful whip of his tail. They screamed in terror as they plummeted to the ground. While the griffins dived to retrieve their owners, Belfynor lowered his body so that it brushed against the parapet.

"Climb on, you three!" he cried.

Christina scrambled onto Belfynor's back, with Sir Owenday and Belatro following closely behind. She soon heard the sound of feet running up the tower stairs. With everyone holding on tightly, the dragon turned around and shot through the air. The queen looked back and saw Lord Evermore and Gilfoit staring at them from the balcony.

"He'll probably send an army after us," she said.

"Don't worry, Your Majesty," Belfynor replied. "I can fly faster than any beast. You'll be in the Well long before they catch up to us."

This reassurance made her relax a bit. Turning her head, she breathed a sigh of relief.

"I must say, Your Majesty, it looks as though you're about to enjoy the shortest reign in the kingdom's history," Eelweed joked.

Christina laughed. "I guess I am," she replied. "But I've learned there are more important things than absolute power and immortality."

CHAPTER TWENTY-THREE
FLIGHT

As Belfynor flew toward the Well Plain, the cool breeze whipped against Christina's face. She thought of Ali and regretted that she hadn't been able to say goodbye to her empyremare. During the flight, she glanced back every now and then to see if anyone was pursuing her, but the pale twilit sky appeared empty.

After flying for an hour, Christina and her companions saw golden grass. But as Belfynor drew closer to her destination, she spotted a large army milling around the Well. Many of the soldiers carried torches, and they resembled little fireflies.

"What are they doing here?" she asked, alarmed.

"Lord Evermore must have put these soldiers there before we came to rescue you," Sir Owenday replied.

Christina felt as though someone had punched her in the stomach. "What are we going to do?" she asked. "Belfy, can you get rid of them?"

"That'll be very difficult without fire, Your Majesty," he replied.

"There must be a thousand soldiers down there," Eelweed said.

Suddenly, there was a flurry of activity on the ground.

"I think we've been spotted," Belatro said as soldiers mounted griffins and flew toward them.

"It's the queen!" a man in a cloak shouted. "Capture her! Don't let her escape! And don't harm her! Kill the others!"

"Where do we go?" Belfynor asked, veering away from the Well. A feeling of hopelessness engulfed Christina. This was even worse than being captured by King James and his soldiers. At least in that instance, she had a refuge to escape to.

"Head for the Kaldewonn Forest!" Sir Owenday replied. "It's only a few miles to the south!"

"You want us to fly in *there*?" Eelweed asked incredulously.

"If we go anywhere else in the kingdom, Lord Evermore's soldiers will simply hunt us down," the knight said. "Perhaps they won't follow us into the Kaldewonn."

"But evil creatures dwell there!" Belatro said.

"We'll be safe as long as we're with Christina," Sir Owenday replied. "The inhabitants won't harm her because she's the queen. At least I hope not."

"This is madness!" Belatro said. "I'd rather be killed by these soldiers than by whatever is in the Kaldewonn!"

"Very well, then we can throw you off this instant and be free of your whining tongue!" Sir Owenday snapped. The jester shut up immediately.

Somewhere in the darkness, they heard a voice cry out, "Shoot the dragon!"

They looked down and saw hundreds of arrows flying toward them. Out of the corner of her eye, Christina spotted a group of soldiers pursuing them in the air. Belfynor banked hard, and Christina could no longer see the soldiers below. She realized that the dragon was protecting his passengers by putting himself between them and the onslaught of arrows.

"What's wrong?" she asked when she heard Belfynor let out an agonized moan. "Are you hit?"

"Yes, Your Majesty," he replied. "One of the soldiers' arrows struck my underbelly. I'm not certain I'll be able to make it all the way to the forest."

"You must!" Sir Owenday said.

"Please, Belfy!" Christina said. "I know you're in a lot of pain right now, but you can do this! I just know it!"

The dragon mustered some energy and shot across the plain, leaving his pursuers far behind. Before long, Christina could see the trees of the Kaldewonn beckoning to her with their spidery arms.

"I can't fly much longer," Belfynor said.

"Try to go deep into the forest," Sir Owenday said. "Stay away from the edge."

The dragon nodded, and when he reached the Kaldewonn, he flew low for a while before landing hard upon the edge of a road made of uneven black stones. His passengers climbed off his back, and Christina thanked him and kissed his snout.

"Where are you hurt?" Sir Owenday asked.

With a great deal of effort, Belfynor rolled over, and his companions saw an arrow sticking out of the lower part of his abdomen.

"I don't think his wound is serious, Your Majesty," Sir Owenday said, "But he should receive immediate medical attention. I know how to treat humans, but not dragons. And I don't have any medical supplies in any case. Do any of you know anything about dragon wounds?"

The others shook their heads.

"We need to find help," Christina said, staring around. The trees here looked as if they had been scorched in a great forest fire; their gnarled black trunks and leafless branches cast a threatening presence. The undergrowth here was sparse, and not a single blade of grass stuck out above the coarse black dirt.

"Well, we've got to do something," Eelweed said.

Belatro pointed toward the trees on the opposite side of the road. "Perhaps these folks can give us aid," he said in a voice full of doubt and irony.

Christina, Sir Owenday, and Eelweed turned around and saw hundreds of hairy brown people approaching with double-edged wooden spears. Their yellow eyes and dog-like teeth made the queen's hair stand on end.

"What are they?" she asked.

"They must be kaldewars, Your Majesty," Sir Owenday said. "I've heard tales about these people, and none of them are pleasant."

"Can they understand what we're saying?"

"I'm not certain."

"It looks as if they would like to have us all for a feast," Eelweed said.

"Quick, Your Majesty!" Sir Owenday said. "Get the Elixir out and let them see it!"

But before she could unstrap her schoolbag, the kaldewars attacked. Christina, Sir Owenday, and Eelweed drew their swords while Belatro ran behind Belfynor's limp body. One of the kaldewars threw his spear aside and jumped at Christina, whose sword training took hold of her. She raised her weapon, and the hapless foe landed on the blade. Then she pulled it out, swung at another attacker, and managed to cut off one of his legs. Over the next few minutes, she and her two comrades slew many kaldewars, who, fortunately, proved to be terribly incompetent fighters. But the attackers' numbers were great, and the defenders soon found themselves overwhelmed. Wanting to be of some use, Belatro picked up a fallen branch and joined the fray.

After Christina killed her ninth kaldewar, she felt hairy hands grab her from behind and pull her to the ground. Another kaldewar put his hands around the blade of her sword and yanked it from her grasp. Rivers of purple blood ran down the creature's fingers, but he didn't seem to mind as he grabbed the hilt and reared back to strike a deadly blow.

From somewhere close by, there came a roar so loud that the trees shook. The kaldewar holding Christina's sword threw it aside, let out a shriek, and scampered away with his comrades. The queen quickly scrambled to her feet and saw a chimera approaching. The monstrous creature possessed the head and body of a lioness and the tail of a snake. A goat's head reared out of the middle of her neck, and her coat was covered in glowing orange embers.

Christina's friends ran for the nearest trees and climbed as high as they could, but she didn't move.

She knew instinctively that this chimera could probably climb trees, or burn them to ashes. After a moment, Sir Owenday climbed down and stood beside her, sword drawn. The chimera walked up to them and roared again. Christina heard her ears ringing. She had never been more terrified in her life; her heart felt as though it would burst from her chest at any moment, but she stood her ground.

After roaring again, the chimera spoke. "What are you trespassers doing on my mistress's road?" she demanded in a deep and terrible voice. "Answer me quickly, or I'll maul you!"

"I-I'm Christina, Queen of Imar," the girl said, holding out the Sword of Etossar.

But the chimera was unimpressed. "Possession of that sword is not proof of your status."

With trembling fingers, Christina unzipped her bag and took out the flask, which glowed a brilliant gold. When the chimera saw this, she bowed her head and said in a gentler voice, "Forgive me, Your Majesty. I'm Charendaya, guardian of this road. Raventir, my mistress, doesn't allow anyone to travel on it unless she grants them permission. She has dominion over this forest, but she must, of course, answer to the ruler of Imar, who is the master of us all."

"My friends have permission to be on this road," Christina said.

Charendaya bowed her head again. "As you wish." She looked over to the trees. "You may come down now, friends of the queen. Neither I nor any other soul in this realm shall harm you."

"Tell that to the creatures who attacked us," Belatro said.

162

"The kaldewars attacked you because they were unaware of the queen's presence," she replied. "Your Majesty, why didn't you show them the flask?"

"I was about to, but they were too quick," Christina said. "I didn't have a chance."

Charendaya nodded. "I see. Well, you're all safe now. Come down from those trees. It must feel uncomfortable up there."

After some hesitation, Eelweed and Belatro climbed to the ground but stayed close to Belfynor.

"Charendaya, can you take me to Raventir?" Christina asked. "We have a dragon here who's injured and needs help right away." She looked around at the others. "Is anyone else hurt?"

The rest of her friends showed minor cuts, but no serious wounds.

"I shall take you to my mistress, Your Majesty," the chimera replied. "You may ride upon my back."

Christina balked at the prospect of touching her scorching flesh. "If I climb on, I'll be burned alive!"

"I do beg your pardon," Charendaya said, and the fire disappeared from her body. "Sometimes I forget I'm aflame. Now you can climb on."

But Christina was reluctant to do this. "What if your back lights up by accident?"

Charendaya laughed. "Don't you know anything about chimeras? We light up at will. Don't worry. You'll be quite safe."

"You must be invincible," Sir Owenday said with awe.

"Oh no, I can be killed," she replied. "But it's very difficult to do so."

"What about my friends?" Christina asked. "What if those kaldewars come back?"

"I'll make a ring of fire around them," Charendaya replied. "The kaldewars hate fire."

"What if the fire spreads?" Eelweed asked.

"Don't be concerned about that, water gnome. It will stay put."

Charendaya's body lit up again, and she blazed a wall of flame around Belfynor, Sir Owenday, Eelweed, and Belatro. When this was done, she walked back to Christina, and her fire faded away. The queen warily climbed on her back, which felt like thick velvet. The goat's head looked down at her and bleated, "Now hold on to my neck."

As soon as Christina did this, Charendaya put on a burst of speed. The queen looked back at her friends, and the flames protecting them grew smaller until disappearing altogether.

CHAPTER TWENTY-FOUR
RAVENTIR

The chimera raced down the road a ways before taking a sharp right into the trees. Night had fallen, but moonlight filtered through the branches. After carrying her passenger through a narrow ravine, Charendaya raced uphill and into a series of tall hedges, and Christina felt as though she were speeding through a labyrinth. When Charendaya finally emerged from the hedge, she stopped in an area with few trees. Christina saw a two-story manor house on a large, barren hill. Made primarily of stone, the house had a wooden roof, and gables of various sizes jutted out at certain points. A stone staircase was built into the hill, and this led up to the front door.

"Here we are, Your Majesty," Charendaya said. "This is where my mistress resides. Hopefully, she is home at the moment. You may want to plug your ears."

Christina put her fingers into her ears a second before the chimera gave a terrible roar, and when she pulled her fingers out, her ears felt as though they had been exposed to a heavy metal concert. After a few moments, a tall, wiry woman wearing a black robe emerged from the house.

"What is it, Charendaya?" the woman asked, giving her long black hair a toss. "Who is that with you?"

"Mistress, I have brought the new queen, and she desires your help," Charendaya replied.

Raventir rushed down the stairs and bowed low before Christina as she introduced herself.

"Your Majesty, I'm pleased to meet you," she said. "I learned of your arrival several weeks ago. So, King James is finally dead?"

"Lord Evermore killed him earlier today," the queen replied, comforted by the kind look in Raventir's brown eyes. "My name's Christina."

"I must say, you're a very brave queen. The rulers usually stay away from this forest, despite their great power."

"I need your help," Christina said. "My friends and I came into the forest to seek refuge. One of them is a dragon, and he has an arrow sticking out of his stomach."

Raventir gave a whistle, and a black horse galloped down the hill. Christina stared at its dagger-sharp teeth and glowing red eyes and knew she had finally found a horse she would never want to ride.

"Don't be afraid, Your Majesty," Raventir said when she saw the look on Christina's face. "Her name is Juliah, and she's very tame."

"What kind of horse is she?"

"A skaromare," Raventir replied, mounting Juliah. "They eat humans, but only grown-ups, so you have nothing to fear. Let's go. We'll fetch Kellomeane. He's my personal warlock."

The group traveled through the forest until they came to a wide hollow formed out of a river that had dried up long ago. Raventir led the other two to the mouth of a large cave.

"Wait here," she said, dismounting from her skaromare. She disappeared into the cave and emerged a few minutes later with a gangly man in a red and white robe. His head was bald, and he reminded Christina of an alien. After Raventir introduced Kellomeane, he came up to Christina and bowed.

"Can you help me?" she asked.

"I think so, Your Majesty," he replied. He and Raventir mounted the skaromare, and they all went back to the road.

***

When they reached the others, the ring of fire still blazed bright. Charendaya blew out the flames while Raventir and Kellomeane dismounted from Juliah. Christina climbed off of the chimera's back and ran over to Belfynor.

"How are you feeling, Belfy?" she asked.

The dragon grinned at her. "I'll live, Your Majesty."

"I'm pleased to meet you, Belfynor," Kellomeane said in a gentle voice. "I'm a warlock, and I'm going to heal you. You'll be back on your feet before long."

He reached into a black leather pouch that hung from his shoulder and produced a dagger. After surveying Belfynor's wound, he said. "I shall have to cut the arrow out. This will hurt, but you're a big dragon, and I'm sure a little pain won't bother you."

Christina noticed that Belfynor was shaking. She felt sorry for him.

"I'm ready," the dragon replied in a voice that suggested otherwise.

Kellomeane went to work with his dagger, and as he carefully removed the arrow from Belfynor's underbelly, the latter gave several ear-splitting roars. When the warlock was finished, he applied some green medicine that he kept in a small phial before sewing up the wounds with Sir Owenday's help.

"We're finished," Kellomeane said, standing up. "Thank you for being such a wonderful patient."

Belfynor whimpered in reply.

"He'll be well in a week or so," Kellomeane said to Christina. "But we'd better take him to my cave to rest."

"But how are we going to get him there?" Eelweed asked. "He's much too heavy for us to carry."

"My kweagels will attend to this," Raventir said. After she gave a shrill whistle, a dozen black-skinned, three-armed men emerged from the trees. Like the waulds, the kweagels stood nine feet, but their cloaks were red instead of black, and long scimitars hung from their belts. Raventir spoke to them in a strange language, and they walked over to Belfynor and lifted him off of the ground.

"After we take the dragon to the cave, the rest of you may come and stay at my house for as long as you wish," Raventir said. "Your Majesty, why don't you ride with me while your friends ride on Charendaya? I wish to speak with you."

Christina reluctantly agreed to this. She was afraid of riding the skaromare but didn't want her host to know that. Raventir turned to Sir Owenday and asked, "Knight, shall I fetch a horse for you?"

"My lady, I'm unable to ride a horse, so I shall walk beside you folks," he replied.

Raventir gave him a strange look before turning to the rest of Christina's friends, who didn't seem eager to mount the chimera. "Don't worry about Charendaya," she said. "You won't burn. She's a perfectly harmless creature...when she wants to be."

Belatro and Eelweed cautiously climbed upon the chimera's back while her master helped Christina up on her skaromare.

***

"May I ask you something, Your Majesty?" Raventir asked as the company made its way among the trees.

"Sure," Christina replied, knowing very well what was coming.

"You mentioned earlier that you and your friends were seeking refuge. But you have the Elixir and the Sword. Are you not aware that you now possess absolute power over the entire kingdom? All you have to do is drink from the flask."

"I know," Christina sighed. "But I want to go home. And it's my right to do so because Ethindir gave that choice to all of the children from my world. But when I refused to drink the Elixir, Lord Evermore and the Order locked me up in a tower and threatened to torture me. And now he's claiming to be the steward and saying I've gone mad and that I'm unfit to rule. But I'm not mad. I just want to be with my mom. I escaped with the help of my friends, but when we got to the Well, there was an army guarding it. I thought the Order was supposed to help me. I thought they were my friends."

"Their actions don't surprise me at all," Raventir said. "Doubtless, the Prophecy has exerted a great deal of influence over Lord Evermore and the Order, but even if there was no prophecy, they would still do everything in their power to prevent you from returning to the World Below. Like most Imarians, they're dependent on the Cycle of Royal Succession. And they covet the immortality that their precious medallions confer upon them."

"Do you want the Cycle to keep going?" Christina held her breath after she asked this question, for she knew that the answer would determine whether or not she would have any chance of going home.

"It matters not to me whether it continues or ends," Raventir replied. "My life will go on as before. My well-being doesn't hinge upon a monarch who lives far away in some castle."

"Is it true you're a powerful enchantress?"

Raventir laughed. "I'm an enchantress, but not very powerful. I can do a few minor spells, and that's the extent of my abilities. I'm much handier with a sword."

"You're not going to hand me over to Lord Evermore, are you?"

"Of course not. As I told you before, you and your friends are welcome to stay in my house. You'll all be safe there. The forest has thousands of trees that will kill on my command and are impervious to fire. If Lord Evermore and his soldiers enter the Kaldewonn, they'll pay dearly for their mistake."

"So you don't believe the Prophecy will come to pass?" Christina asked as she looked up into Raventir's face.

The enchantress shook her head. "I've always thought the Prophecy was absurd. Eternal peace exists in the netherworld, not this one."

"Can you help me then? Could you launch an attack on the army around the Well tonight?"

"It will take me a week or so to gather my forces. By that time, Lord Evermore will have amassed a huge army around the Well. No, if you wish to return home, you'll need more soldiers than I can provide. As soon as you're settled in my house, I shall dispatch kaldewar messengers to travel the kingdom and summon all loyal humans and creatures to your side. Most Imarians will probably join Lord Evermore and attempt to prevent the Cycle from ending, but some may come over to us. Those willing to fight for you will be promised safety in this forest."

Christina nodded. "Thank you for helping me."

"You're welcome, Your Majesty."

***

By the time the company reached Kellomeane's cave, Belfynor was in a deep slumber. Once the kweagels carried him inside, Christina thanked the warlock for his help and said goodnight. Then she and the rest of the company rode back to Raventir's home. The enchantress led Christina and her friends into the house and up a narrow spiral staircase to their rooms. When the queen reached hers, she flopped down on the bed and fell asleep.

CHAPTER TWENTY-FIVE
THE COUNCIL

On the following morning, Raventir's messengers mounted griffins and flew around the kingdom to persuade Imarians to join the queen. At the same time, Lord Evermore—who had flown to the Well immediately after Christina's escape—dispatched his own messengers. Christina's messengers argued that she, as the rightful ruler, had command over every soldier in the kingdom. Lord Evermore's messengers argued, however, that since Christina was unfit to rule due to her apparent madness—for no human or creature in a proper state of mind would refuse immortality and absolute power—this made him Steward of Imar. They also said that the Eternal Ruler would never arrive if Christina destroyed the Well.

As Raventir predicted, the prospect of the Cycle's end horrified most Imarians, and they sided with Lord Evermore, who quickly assembled a vast army and placed it around the Well. Even so, many humans, water gnomes, waulds, dwarfs, celestonirs, and other creatures gave their allegiance to the queen and set up an encampment in the area of the Well Plain that bordered the Kaldewonn Forest.

To Christina's delight, Lord Bodwar, Hymral, and Helvondir came to give their support. However, Sir Kranwick and the miniatures never appeared. This hurt Christina, but she understood; the glass knight and his countrymen probably blamed her for missing the Battle of the Amber Castle. She hoped they hadn't joined Lord Evermore.

Christina and Sir Owenday continued with her sword training and were pleased to discover that she was making a great deal of progress. The queen often went to the encampment to visit with her soldiers, and whenever she left the safety of Raventir's home, her friends went along to protect her from any danger or treachery.

After a week had passed since her escape to the Kaldewonn Forest, Christina asked Lord Bodwar to conduct a head count of all her soldiers and sent two celestonirs named Ariondel and Arwyndel to the enemy's camp to gather information. When these tasks were finished, the queen convened a war council, which was held late at night in a giant tent near her encampment. The participants included Christina, Lord Bodwar, Raventir, Kellomeane, Hymral, Sir Owenday, Eelweed, Belatro, Helvondir, Ariondel, Arwyndel, and Belfynor. They all sat on wooden stools in a circle except for the dragon, who poked his head through the flap.

After thanking everyone for coming, the queen said, "Lord Bodwar, how many soldiers do I have?"

"Around twenty-five thousand," he replied.

"And one dragon," Belfynor piped in.

Christina nodded before turning to her spies and asking, "What have you learned of Lord Evermore's plans? Is he going to launch an attack? And how many soldiers does *he* have?"

Ariondel cleared his throat before speaking.

"Lord Evermore is staying put. He's afraid of taking any of his soldiers away from the Well. And he realizes that even if he attacked, we'd just retreat into the Kaldewonn, where we have the advantage. Lord Evermore is counting on you to take the offensive. He knows you can't keep your army together forever. Your soldiers joined this camp because they believe that you possess the authority to command, but many of them don't wish to see the Cycle end any more than the Order does, and if you don't act soon, their inner feelings may compel them to join with the enemy."

"Then I guess I'll have to start the battle," the queen replied. "I'm afraid to ask, but how many soldiers does Lord Evermore have around the Well?"

"His army numbers seventy-five thousand," Arwyndel said, massaging one his wings.

Christina blanched. "*Seventy-five thousand?*"

"This is great news, Your Majesty!" Belatro said.

Sir Owenday rounded on the jester. "And what, pray tell me, could possibly be great about being outnumbered three to one?" he asked angrily.

"When our worst archers shoot their arrows, they'll be more likely to hit something," Belatro replied with a grin.

The others shook their heads.

"We need to come up with a strategy to get to that Well," the queen said. "Any ideas?"

An uneasy silence settled upon the group before Hymral spoke up.

"Your Majesty, strategies aimed at overcoming enormous odds in battle haven't been employed for thousands of years," she said. "The battles of rebellion and royal succession are the only ones waged in Imar, and the armies of the former rulers are always outnumbered. When we took the Amber Castle, we paid a heavy toll, but our victory was assured because King James only possessed a thousand soldiers while we had fifty times that number. And after the new rulers take the throne, they wield the awesome power of the Sword of Etossar."

"But I'm not trying to defeat Lord Evermore's army," Christina said. "I just need to reach the Well. Can we tunnel our way to it?"

"I'm afraid not," Lord Bodwar replied. "The plain is enchanted ground. On the other hand, Lord Evermore can't build anything around the Well or seal it up."

"It seems to me, Your Majesty," Hymral said, "That the quickest way to reach the Well is by air. I and my two thousand celestonir warriors could get you there in a timely manner."

"And I have my flying cavalry," Helvondir said. "We tree gnomes may be small, but we're fierce fighters. And the antlers of our perytons can pierce any armor."

"And don't forget about me," Belfynor said. "I may not be able to produce fire, but with Hymral's and Helvondir's soldiers at my side, we'll be more than a match for Lord Evermore's army in the sky. Your Majesty, since you no longer have an empyremare, will you permit me to be your means of flight? The enemy will think twice about coming near you during the battle."

"I would be honored, Belfy," she replied.

"Then it's settled," Hymral said. "We'll fly Christina to the Well."

"But even if you manage to accomplish that, you'll still have to contend with Lord Evermore's army on the ground," Belatro said. "You can't simply drop the queen into the Well; the portal requires some time to open. You'll have to take the Well and keep the enemy at bay long enough to allow Her Majesty to go through unmolested."

"We'll use our ground force as a diversion," Hymral replied. "We have twenty thousand foot and cavalry soldiers. They can draw most of Lord Evermore's soldiers away from the Well."

Sir Owenday spoke up. "Your Majesty, perhaps we can use them for something more than a mere diversion. Perhaps they can reach the Well itself."

"But how could they achieve such an end against an army that's much larger?" Eelweed asked.

Christina pondered this for a moment.

"Hold on a second," she said. "I think I have an idea. Haroldine the Great conquered other kingdoms by defeating larger armies. I read about her campaigns at the library in the Sanctuary. One time, she took an army of ten thousand soldiers into battle against an army of fifty thousand. She arranged her soldiers into a hollow triangle and placed her best infantrymen and archers in front to break the center of the enemy force, and she put her other infantry and archer battalions on the wings. She also placed her cavalry in the rear and on the flanks to provide protection and attack the enemy once their flanks were exposed. When Haroldine's army went into battle, it smashed through the other army and broke it apart, and she won. We could try the same thing. And our army in the air can support the one on the ground."

Sir Owenday stroked his beard as he pondered Christina's idea. "This might work," he said at last.

"I think this is a good plan," Raventir said. "With the combined strength of all our forces, we may be able to pull it off."

"How far away is the Well?" Christina asked.

"Five miles if we advance northward from this camp," Lord Bodwar replied.

She nodded. "Tell the soldiers that we'll attack Lord Evermore's army in three days."

The meeting ended shortly afterward and everyone retired to bed.

***

The next morning, Christina and her friends were eating breakfast in Raventir's dining room when Lord Bodwar came in and announced that an emissary from Lord Evermore had arrived at the encampment bearing a white flag.

"Your Majesty, he says Lord Evermore desires to have a parley with you this evening at seven o'clock," Lord Bodwar said.

"What does he want?"

"He wouldn't say."

"Don't do it, Your Majesty," Sir Owenday said. "It's bound to be a trick."

"The emissary swears that Lord Evermore makes this offer in good faith," Lord Bodwar said. "And to show he means well, the Head of the Order will come

177

alone to our camp. He shall be unarmed, but you may bring your sword to the meeting. He only requests that you not harm him."

Christina thought about this for a minute. She didn't wish to have anything to do with the man who had locked her up in a tower and threatened her with torture, but she was curious to hear what he had to say. Finally, she said, "Tell that emissary I'll meet with Lord Evermore right outside our camp at seven tonight."

Lord Bodwar bowed his head and left to relay the message.

CHAPTER TWENTY-SIX
THE PARLEY

Christina, Sir Owenday, Eelweed, and Belatro arrived at the rendezvous a few minutes before the meeting was scheduled to begin. Lord Evermore came at exactly seven o'clock, and he was followed by a familiar-looking animal.

"Ali!" Christina cried out, and the empyremare whinnied and trotted over to her. The queen buried her face in the golden mane.

"Your Majesty, I've brought her here as a gesture of good will," Lord Evermore said.

Christina looked up at him and quickly suppressed her emotions, for she suspected that the Head of the Order had returned her empyremare in an attempt to manipulate her. Instead of thanking him, she blurted out, "What do you want?"

Lord Evermore didn't reply at first but sat upon the golden grass. Sighing, Christina followed suit so that she could look him in the face. Ali bent her head down and nuzzled the queen's cheek while she stroked her empyremare's nose. Sir Owenday, Eelweed, and Belatro stood behind Christina and kept a close watch on Lord Evermore; the knight and the water gnome had their swords at the ready in case of trouble.

"I've come to make one last attempt to reason with you," the Head of the Order said. "And I also bring a warning. I know that you're going to attempt to reach the Well of Rulers, and my spies inform me that you have twenty-five thousand soldiers under your command. Doubtless, you have sent spies into my camp and must be aware that my army numbers seventy-five thousand. I want you to know that if you continue with your plan, we'll kill not only you, but every one of your soldiers, regardless of whether or not you reach the Well."

"Ethindir gave me the choice to stay or leave," Christina replied. "And I'm leaving."

"But the great sorcerer would never have given this choice so freely if he had known about the Prophecy."

"You know something?" Christina said, and her voice grew more agitated with every word. "I don't think there really is an Eternal Ruler! I think you made up the Prophecy as an excuse to go against Ethindir's wishes and force children to stay in the kingdom!"

Lord Evermore shook his head.

"Your words come from anger, not truth," he said. His voice remained calm, and this made the queen angrier. "I have never made a false prediction. But even if you were correct about the Prophecy, the Cycle should still continue. Ethindir was wrong to make the Well's destruction a possibility, and it's up to the Order to preserve Imar. The Cycle's power has held this great kingdom together for thousands of years. If you accomplish your goal, Imar will break apart, and all of its inhabitants shall be at the mercy of a future that is certain to be much worse than the past. But I can see that I'm making no progress with you. Very well, Your Majesty. I shall see you on the Well Plain. Ever since you arrived in the kingdom, you've been nothing but a hindrance."

"At least I'm not like you!" she replied. "I don't force innocent children into a cycle that destroys their souls and then their lives!"

"I am not an evil man," Lord Evermore said, still calm. "Did I not tell you that I'm trying to rid this kingdom of evil? If we in the Order must employ unsavory means to achieve our ends, then such is justified for the sake of the kingdom. And don't act so noble, Your Majesty. You'll have Imarians die for a selfish cause."

"How can *I* be selfish?" she asked, her face growing red. "I want to give up absolute power and immortality! You're the selfish one! You'll have Imarians die just so you and your friends in the Order can live forever!"

He laughed. "Your Majesty, I assure you, I only want to give power to children from the World Below so that my fellow Imarians can continue to live in a great and peaceful kingdom. My immortality is but small recompense for the dangers and hardships I face while fulfilling my duty to Imar. Yes, humans and creatures will perish under my command, but they shall do so for the greater good. You, on the other hand, are willing to have others die so that *you* may live the life *you* desire."

Christina had no reply to this. She just sat there and let his words sink in. Lord Evermore stood up and shook some loose dirt and grass from his golden robe.

"Come toward the Well if you wish," he said, "But you shall fail. The Cycle *will* continue, and the Eternal Ruler will come."

***

Later that night, Christina tossed and turned in her bed. What a terrible choice she faced! If she drank the Elixir, there would be no war, and the kingdom would continue to enjoy peace. But she would probably come to the same dismal end that had befallen other children from her world. Yet, if she waged war against the Order, thousands of Imarians would perish on her behalf, and they would likely do so in vain, for there was little chance of her reaching the Well. And even if she managed to destroy it and go home, she would never be able to live with the knowledge that she had pushed others to their deaths for the sake of her own happiness.

By the following morning, Christina came to a decision. It was the least terrible one she faced, and she was ready to accept the consequences.

CHAPTER TWENTY-SEVEN
THE ROYAL DECREE

After breakfast, Christina asked Raventir for a pencil and paper. Since these items were not available, one of the enchantress's kaldewar servants fetched a piece of yellow parchment and a quill, and the queen spent the next several hours writing out a royal decree. She was amused by the fact that this was to be her first decree—and her last. When she finished, she summoned Raventir, Sir Owenday, Lord Bodwar, and Hymral to her room.

"I've written out a royal decree, and I want to read it to all of my soldiers and friends," she said. "Can you guys assemble my army? And can someone get me something to stand on?"

They nodded and left to carry out her requests.

When Christina arrived at the encampment with her friends and empyremare, her soldiers were gathered together and awaiting her speech. The overcast sky reflected her gloom. Two kweagels took a giant boulder from the forest and placed it in front of the throng of Imarians. After Sir Owenday helped her onto the rock, the queen looked out at the sea of faces and steeled herself. When everyone was quiet, she held the decree before her with shaking hands and began to read aloud.

"First, I want to thank you all for leaving your homes and coming to my aid," she said in a tremulous voice. "Most of you are aware by now that we're greatly outnumbered by Lord Evermore's army. Last night, he visited our camp and attempted to persuade me to change my mind. During our discussion, he told me that his army will kill any Imarian who fights at my side. I've given the matter a lot of thought and have decided that I'm still going to try to reach the Well tomorrow and destroy it. However, I've also decided that I can't force others to die for my own choices. I made a terrible mistake coming here in the first place, but I shouldn't expect any of you to pay for that. So as of this moment, I release all of you from my service."

Gasps and murmurs rippled through her audience.

"But before you go," she continued, "I have one royal decree to make, which is this: You are all to go and live wonderful, fulfilling lives."

Tears brimming, Christina dropped the parchment and jumped down from the rock. She mounted Ali and rode back to Raventir's home by herself.

***

Despite her dire situation, a great burden had been lifted from her shoulders. Her decision was the only logical one, and she felt better for doing what she believed was right. Determined to pursue her intended course of action and hoping for a miracle, she had no illusions as to what was likely to happen.

When Christina reached the bottom of the stone staircase that led up to Raventir's house, she dismounted from her empyremare. She spent the next several minutes hugging Ali's neck while the empyremare gently nuzzled her face. After forcing herself to let go, Christina looked into those loving sapphire eyes and said, "Goodbye, girl. You can't come any further with me. I couldn't bear it if you were hurt or killed tomorrow. And besides, you belong in your world. Fly back to the Oranbeorosphere. I just want you to know I've enjoyed our rides together, and no matter what happens, I'll always love you and remember you."

Ali nodded her head as if to say that she understood. After nuzzling Christina's face one last time, the empyremare turned around, trotted a few steps, and launched herself into the air. As she flew toward her home in the skies, Ali turned her head to give Christina one final look of affection. When her empyremare disappeared from view, the queen sat on the lowest stone step and had a good cry. As she rose to go up to the house, someone above her called out her name in a harsh, guttural voice. Looking up, she saw Belfynor flying toward her with Raventir, Sir Owenday, Eelweed, and Belatro on his back. When the dragon landed in front of the queen, the others climbed off and gathered around her.

"Your Majesty, why didn't you tell us what you were going to do before making that speech to everyone?" Raventir demanded.

"Yes," Sir Owenday said. "You might have mentioned it to your friends beforehand."

"Sorry about that," Christina replied. "I was afraid you would try to talk me out of it."

"You're right, we would have," Belatro said. "Why are you going to the Well by yourself? That's madness! You'll be dead long before you set your eyes upon it."

"If I made others sacrifice their lives on my account and managed to get home, I'd never be able to live with myself," Christina replied. "But if I fled this place, Lord Evermore and the Order would find me sooner or later."

"Where's Ali?" Eelweed asked.

"I let her go," Christina replied. "I had to. I couldn't bring her with me and see her killed."

"Your Majesty, we came to tell you that you won't be alone when you face Lord Evermore and his army," Belfynor said. "We're going with you, even if you refuse to take us. Ever since you arrived in the kingdom, you've enriched all of our lives."

"That's right," Eelweed added. "Because of you, I've gone on exciting adventures, beheld amazing sights, and made the best friends a water gnome could ever hope for."

"And I finally have a ruler who's worth serving," Belatro said.

"The least we can do is help you return to your own world," Sir Owenday said. "We love you, not because you're our queen, but because you're our friend. And we all think you're worth fighting for, and even dying for."

The others nodded in agreement.

"Thanks, everyone," Christina sniffed, overcome with joy at hearing the words she had longed for. "And you can quit calling me 'Your Majesty.' My name is 'Christina'."

"Yes, Your Majesty!" they all replied.

"My warriors are coming, too," Raventir said. "They'll be handy in the battle, for they enjoy killing and have no fear of death."

"And pay no heed to what Lord Evermore told you," Belatro said. "You aren't selfish, but selfless. If you destroy the Well, you'll do so not only for yourself, but for all the children of the World Below."

"I really appreciate all the help," Christina said, "But we still don't have enough soldiers to fight Lord Evermore's army. We need a miracle."

"And we may now have one," Belfynor said. "Earlier today, I told Kellomeane about my lung disorder, and he said he possessed the information and the tools to fix it and would perform the operation. He's going to begin first thing tomorrow morning. I was going to tell you this tonight, but now is a better time. Kellomeane also told me that the operation may take a while, so you'll want to delay your attack."

"Alright," Christina replied. "I'll do it. I'm awfully glad you finally found a warlock who'll perform the operation, but even if you can breathe fire, we'll still be up against great odds."

"Don't be pessimistic, Christina," Raventir said in a kind but firm voice. "Maintain a positive outlook and everything will turn out all right. You're going to see your mother again. I promise you. We're going to help you reach that Well. No matter what it takes, we'll get you home."

187

CHAPTER TWENTY-EIGHT
THE THREE MIRACLES

On the following morning, Kellomeane came to the house to fetch Belfynor. Christina had never seen the dragon look so anxious. His entire body quaked, and waterfalls of sweat ran down the sides of his head. Her heart ached for him.

"Do you want me to keep you company?" she asked.

"Please do," he replied.

So Christina accompanied her reptilian friend to the warlock's cave. Kellomeane made Belfynor lie flat on his stomach—a difficult task due to the dragon's recent wound—and propped his mouth open with a heavy stone slab. Belfynor had to remain in this uncomfortable state for a whole day and night while Kellomeane worked on his lungs. The warlock used many sharp utensils, but he gave Belfynor a potion that dulled the pain. Christina sat with him through most of the ordeal and caressed the side of his leathery face.

Kellomeane's robes were scorched a few times during the operation, but he finished his work with no real harm done. After cleaning out the blood from the dragon's throat and mouth and washing his hands, he said, "It's all over, Belfynor. Once again, you've been a model patient. Now you're going to feel some pain and discomfort over the next few days, but that's natural. Do not speak or attempt to breathe fire for seventy-two hours. That's very important. When the time period has elapsed, we shall see if the operation was successful. Nod your head if you understand me."

With a great deal of effort, the dragon bobbed his head up and down.

"Good. You can remain in my cave and rest. Your Majesty, you may stay too if you like."

***

When the time came to test the results of the operation, Kellomeane and Christina led Belfynor out of the cave and were surprised to see Raventir, Sir Owenday, Eelweed, and Belatro waiting for them.

"This is it, my good dragon," the warlock said. "I've done everything I can. Now let's see if our efforts bore any fruit. Try not to be too disappointed if you still can't breathe fire."

Trembling, Belfynor took a slow, deep breath. After several tense seconds, he rapidly exhaled, and a brilliant bluish-green flame shot from his mouth. Everyone clapped and cheered.

"Hooray!" Christina shouted. "You can do it!"

"Bravo!" Belatro said.

After spewing forth a few more jets of fire, Belfynor turned to Kellomeane and said, "Oh, this is the happiest day of my life! I'm a full-fledged dragon now! I'll be forever indebted to you! You're the greatest warlock in the kingdom!"

"You're welcome," Kellomeane replied. "But I was simply doing my job."

"I'll have none of that!" Belfynor said. "No other warlock would help me. But *you* did. And Christina, if you hadn't convinced me to come out of my lair, this great miracle would never have happened. So I'm indebted to you as well, and to show my eternal gratitude, I'm going to give both of you a very special dragon hug!"

"Run!" she shouted, grabbing Kellomeane's hand and trying to pull him away. But it was too late. Belfynor grabbed the two humans and lifted them up to his chest for an embrace. When he finally put them back on the ground, they both looked as if they had been squeezed into tin cans.

"I'm glad your dreams have come true, my friend," Sir Owenday said to Belfynor, who danced with joy. "I only wish mine could, too."

"What do you desire, Sir Knight?" Raventir asked.

"I wish to ride again," he replied wistfully. "Many years ago, a witch cursed me so that I couldn't sit on a horse. You see, I was out riding one night and saw her walking a good distance in front of me, so I decided to keep going and force her off the road. I was a very cruel and arrogant young man, and intoxicated much of the time. But I didn't mean to trample her. I assumed she would move out of the way before I hit her. Well, she moved all right. At the last moment, the witch stepped aside and shot a curse in my direction. It hit me in the back of the head, and the witch disappeared before I knew what had happened. I looked everywhere for her, but in vain. It served me right, though. At first, I felt sorry because I'd been cursed. But over time, I became sorry for the way I treated others."

After pondering this for a moment, Raventir said, "Sir Knight, I think I may have been the one who put that curse on you."

Sir Owenday gaped. "It was *you*?"

"Yes," she replied. "You see, I perfected that particular curse when I was a young girl, for I was infatuated with magic. I only know a few spells, and that's one of them. I grew up the daughter of a nobleman, and he tried to marry me off to a dull, witless baron, so I rebelled and ran away from home the day before the wedding. When he discovered I was missing, my father sent several knights to find me. I ended up fleeing to this forest, but during my journey, I saw you coming down the road in my direction. I shot the curse at your head because I mistook you for one of my pursuers. I apologize for the mistake, but you were awfully fortunate I didn't know an even worse spell."

"My lady, you have nothing to apologize for," Sir Owenday said. "I deserved that curse. Now will you accept *my* apology?"

Raventir smiled. "I do. And I shall take your curse off. Kneel before me and remove your helmet."

Sir Owenday did as he was told, and it occurred to Christina that she had never seen her bodyguard without his helmet on. He had beautiful, curly black hair, but on the back of his head, she noticed a round bald spot covered by a purple mark resembling a small gash. Raventir put her hand over it and softly mouthed some strange words. When she pulled her hand away, the mark began to glow a fiery red, and as it slowly disappeared, hair grew in its place.

"There you are," Raventir said. "The curse has been lifted."

Sir Owenday rose slowly to his feet and felt the back of his head.

"Thank you!" he said. "Now I need a horse to ride."

"Wait here," the enchantress replied. "I shall fetch you one."

She went away and returned a few minutes later with a skaromare. Sir Owenday put his helmet back on and lowered the visor.

"His name is Rodumonn," Raventir said as she handed over the reins. "He's pretty friendly for a member of his species, but you should probably stay clear of his teeth."

Sir Owenday wanted so badly to ride again that he didn't even blink at the prospect of mounting a man-eating horse. He climbed upon Rodumonn's back but fell off the other side.

"Are you okay?" Eelweed asked, an alarmed look on her face.

"Yes," Sir Owenday replied. "Don't worry about me. That one was merely practice. This one's for real."

He rose and mounted the skaromare again but immediately lost his balance and fell backwards onto the ground. Christina ran over to help the knight, but he held up his hand and said, "It's quite all right. I'm only a little rusty."

"No pun intended!" Belatro called out before collapsing to the ground in a fit of uncontrollable giggling.

Sir Owenday cautiously pulled himself up onto Rodumonn's back for a third try. The knight tensed as though expecting to be thrown into the air, but when nothing happened, he grabbed the reins and whooped with joy as he and the horse raced around the hollow. Upon returning to the company, an ecstatic Sir Owenday thanked Raventir by kissing her hand.

"How would you like to ride into battle with my headless knights and I?" she asked him.

Christina, Eelweed, and Belatro let out a collective gasp.

"*You have knights without heads?*" the jester asked.

Raventir nodded, an amused look on her smooth face. "I have several thousand of them under my command."

"How do they talk?" Eelweed asked.

"Their eyes, noses, and mouths are located on their chests," the enchantress replied matter-of-factly.

"My lady, I would be honored to ride with you and your knights," Sir Owenday said. "But as Christina's personal bodyguard, I should stay at her side and protect her as best I can."

"Go ahead," Christina said. "If you're fighting in my army, then you're still protecting me. And you might not get another chance to ride into battle. We may all be killed. Belfynor's fire will help a lot, but we still have a small army to fight with."

"Not as small as you think, Your Majesty," someone said from behind Christina. She turned around and saw a large grizzly bear lumbering toward her.

"Lord Bodwar!" she cried. "What are you doing here?"

193

"I have something to show you. Come."

He led Christina and the others over to the encampment on the edge of the Well Plain, where she found her army. The queen was shocked. She had assumed that her soldiers had departed for their homes or even joined Lord Evermore upon being released from her service.

"What's going on here?" she demanded. "I let everyone go."

Lord Bodwar turned into a man and said, "After you left, we decided to fight for you anyway."

"You mean all of the soldiers chose to stay?" she asked in disbelief.

He nodded his head.

"But why?"

"Because you were willing to sacrifice your life so that none of your subjects would come to harm," he replied with a smile. "No other monarch has ever done this. All of your predecessors valued their lives above ours. That's understandable, of course. But you are different, and we've all concluded that while you may not be the Eternal Ruler, you're still a ruler like no other. And when your soldiers march into battle with you, they'll do so of their own free will."

When word spread that the queen had arrived, Imarians came up to her to give homage, but she unexpectedly grasped their hands and shook them. Eelweed and Belatro hoisted Christina on their shoulders and paraded her around the camp. This delighted the soldiers, who cheered and cried out, "Long live Queen Christina!" As she grinned and waved, she pondered the irony that by releasing her soldiers, she had increased their loyalty beyond all proportion.

When she finally returned to the ground, Christina told Lord Bodwar to inform everybody that the attack would take place the next morning.

**

She and the others decided to spend the night with the army and returned to Raventir's house to pack. While in her bedroom, she called for Eelweed and Belatro.

"A lot of Imarians are going to get killed tomorrow, and there's no point in you two risking your lives for my sake," she said. "I know you were planning to go with me, and I really appreciate that, but I have my army again, and Belfy can breathe fire. I stand a decent chance of getting home, so maybe we should say goodbye right now."

"Christina, we're riding with you, and that's final," Eelweed replied. "You may think you're going to be all right now, but you may need us tomorrow."

"You're not going to be free of us that easily," Belatro said with a grin.

"Alright," she sighed. "But if we get into the battle and you decide you don't like getting shot at by every arrow in Lord Evermore's army, don't blame me."

Later that evening in the encampment, as Christina prepared her bed, she heard the tent flap open and turned around to see two familiar faces.

"Metorah! Fryndain!" she cried out. The polevicks gave a stiff bow, but she embraced them, and they didn't bristle this time. "It's so great to see you! Where's Erinonda?"

"Back at our village, Your Majesty," Metorah replied. "We heard the news and hastened here to fight for our queen."

"That's very nice of you," she replied, "But shouldn't you be with your clan?"

"Do you not remember what we told you before we parted company at the mountains?" Fryndain said, rubbing the back of his bald head. "You are a member of our family. I told father that we had a duty to come to your aid, and he agreed."

Feeling too overwhelmed to respond, Christina gave the polevicks another hug.

The soldiers held a feast for Christina that night. She tried to enjoy the affair, but as the hours wore on, the upcoming battle weighed heavily on her mind. She was glad to have an army to fight with again, but this was little comfort, for she knew that a greater force waited only a few miles away and would stop at nothing to destroy her.

CHAPTER TWENTY-NINE
BEAUTIFUL MORNING

When she awoke at dawn, Christina dug into her schoolbag and pulled out the clothes she had worn the day she left home. The queen decided to put these on before donning her tunic, leggings, boots, and chainmail, but she trembled so much that Eelweed and Belatro had to help her dress. The army enjoyed a hearty breakfast, but she couldn't swallow a mouthful because it felt like strong invisible hands were squeezing her insides. The weather was sunny and clear, but for Christina, the coming fight cast a pall over this otherwise beautiful day.

When the meal was over, the queen escaped to her tent for a private moment while her army prepared for battle. For the thousandth time, she checked to make sure the Sword of Etossar was in its scabbard and the flask of Elixir was in her schoolbag. Hearing the flap open, she looked up and saw Raventir. Black armor covered the enchantress from head to toe. Even her sword and shield were the color of night.

"Wow!" the queen said.

Raventir smiled. "How are you feeling, Christina?"

"Awful," she replied, flinging her arms around the enchantress's waist. "I'm afraid to die."

Raventir wrapped her own wiry arms around the queen's shoulders. "You're not going to die. At least not today. You and your mother are going to be reunited. I can see why your friends love you as much as they do. You must have been a wonderful person back in your world."

"No, I wasn't," Christina said with a laugh. "I was a spoiled brat. If I make it home, I'll try every day to be a better person. Raventir, something's been bothering me lately. When I talked with Lord Evermore, he said the kingdom would break apart if I destroyed the Well. Is that true?"

The enchantress nodded. "Without a powerful and immortal ruler, dissolution is the most likely outcome. But nothing is eternal in this world. If you didn't destroy the Well, then someone else would. Imar may have lasted much longer than any other kingdom in Myredan, but no kingdom can last forever."

"What will happen after the kingdom breaks up?"

"I can't say. A number of smaller kingdoms could emerge, or something completely new may arise from the ashes of Imar. We shall have to wait and see what the future has in store for this land. You know, Christina, if you succeed, Lord Evermore's prophecy will still come true."

"What do you mean?"

Raventir recited:

> "When the One ascends to power,
> The Elixir shall never sour.
> So comes the Cycle's final hour."

The enchantress continued. "When King James died, you ascended to power and became our queen. And when you destroy the Well, the Elixir will never darken, and you'll have a chance to live a life free of evil. And the Cycle will be broken forever."

Christina laughed. "I guess you're right. But that's not how most Imarians will see it. And I don't think the Prophecy is genuine anyway."

"I don't think it is either," Raventir replied, smiling. "But you can make it come to pass, only not in the way Lord Evermore intended."

***

Before long, Christina's army was ready for battle. Her ground soldiers arranged themselves into a hollow triangle. The waulds stood at the front, their wooden pikes pointing upward and forming a leafless forest. Polevick cavalry on minicorns were placed on either side of the waulds. These two groups made up the spearhead of the ground army, while Charendaya and Lord Bodwar—presently in human form—occupied the tip. Kaldewar and kweagel infantry and water gnome cavalrymen on dragon turtles formed the right flank, while human and dwarf infantry and headless knights on skaromares formed the left. Mace-wielding ogres and human knights on horses brought up the rear. Tree gnomes on perytons, humans on griffins, and Belfynor occupied the center of the triangle while celestonirs hovered above. To distinguish themselves from their foes, the queen's soldiers wore black armbands with a large white "C" painted on them.

Christina, Eelweed, and Belatro said goodbye to Kellomeane and made their way through the ranks to Belfynor. As the trio passed the polevick warriors, the queen gave Metorah and Fryndain another hug. And when they reached Sir Owenday and Raventir, sitting on their skaromares at the front of the headless column, they stopped and wished the two of them luck.

"Take care of yourselves," Raventir said.

"And may fortune shine upon all of us," Sir Owenday added.

"In case I don't ever see you again, I just want you to know that I think you're the best knight in the kingdom," Christina said to her bodyguard in a choking voice.

In response, Sir Owenday dismounted from Rodumonn and gave the queen a hug. When he remounted, she followed Eelweed and Belatro to the center of the army. After they were all seated on Belfynor's back, the dragon turned his head to look at her and asked, "Are you ready, Christina?"

"I'm as ready as I'll ever be," she replied. "Forward, Imarians!"

The soldiers gave a thunderous reply, and the army started its advance.

CHAPTER THIRTY
ON THE PLAIN OF ETHINDIR

As the army moved slowly across the plain, Belfynor and the other flying beasts walked with the rest of the ground soldiers; only the celestonirs traveled in the air. Christina's feeling of dread grew with every passing mile. Halfway to the Well, she called for a brief rest, and after fifteen minutes, the advance resumed.

When Christina and her soldiers left their encampment, Lord Evermore's forces reacted immediately, taking up position around the Well. His ground soldiers, numbering sixty-five thousand, left their tents and arranged themselves into dense formations while ten thousand of their comrades flew into the air on wings or beasts. Christina's army, which advanced from the south, faced legions of humans, waulds, and dwarfs. Each enemy soldier wore a black armband with a golden ouroboros symbol on it. All of the Order members, save for Lord Evermore, surrounded the Well itself. Strangely, the Head of the Order was nowhere to be seen.

When the queen's soldiers were several hundred yards away from the enemy, Belfynor said, "Christina, do you wish me to turn back? Because I can if you want."

"No," Christina replied in a grim voice. She had braced herself for this moment, but when she saw Lord Evermore's army, her stomach gave a lurch, and she was thankful she hadn't eaten any breakfast.

"Hang on, everybody!" Belfynor said, flapping his wings and taking flight. The other flying beasts in the queen's army quickly followed suit.

"Forth, Imarians!" Lord Bodwar bellowed in his deep bearlike voice. "To the Well of Rulers! For Queen Christina! Let's get her home lads! *Long live the queen!*"

Every one of her soldiers raised their weapons and cried, *"Long live the queen!"*

Lord Bodwar started running toward the enemy lines, and his black beard shook to and fro as he puffed along. Charendaya followed closely behind him, and the rest of the army surged forward with increasing speed. Moments later, Lord Evermore's archers blanketed the sky with arrows; at the same time, the queen's archers loosed a volley of their own. The sight of arrows hurtling toward her caused Christina to duck her head. Belfynor managed to avoid being hit, but others weren't so fortunate. As she watched humans and creatures plummet to their deaths, the queen briefly pondered the cruel irony of her situation—she possessed the power to destroy her enemies in a single blow, but using that very power would spell her own defeat and seal her fate.

As Christina's ground army drew closer to the Order's legions, the polevicks shot arrows in rapid succession at the humans in the center of the opposing force and created a narrow gap in their lines. When Lord Bodwar was about ten feet away from the enemy, he made a flying leap and transformed into a bear in midair. Landing on some soldiers, he began tearing them to pieces. At the same time, Charendaya's body burst aflame, and she charged into a group of hapless foes who had no means of escape except a fiery death.

The waulds lowered their pikes and thrust them into the enemy's densely packed ranks. The polevicks took up their own spears and brought down many enemies while the minicorns stabbed and slashed with their spiral horns. Soon the entire weight and power of the queen's ground force smashed into the Order's legions. It made rapid progress at first but slowed down as casualties mounted and enemy soldiers from other positions rushed over to join the fight. Soon, the attackers were surrounded on all sides by a force twice as large as their own, and their flanks and rearguard were hammered with brutal intensity. As the combatants fought, clouds of billowing gold dust rose from the ground.

***

In the air, arrows killed hundreds of soldiers and beasts during the opening moments of the battle. Belfynor held his fire until the Order's flying warriors came within range, and when the moment was right, Christina said, "Okay, Belfy! Let'em have it!"

The dragon belched out a burst of flame, hitting a group of enemy soldiers and causing the rest of their comrades to fly out of the way. After this awesome display of firepower, the enemy stayed a good distance from Belfynor. When their arrows were spent, celestonirs, humans, and tree gnomes on both sides drew swords and spears and clashed with each other. Many who died in the air fell upon soldiers fighting on the plain and killed them instantly. After several minutes of intense combat, Christina looked down and said, "Belfy, our friends on the ground are in trouble! We've got to help them!"

As the dragon flew toward the battle raging below, Helvondir shouted, "Look out!" Belfynor glanced behind him and swerved so sharply to the right that his passengers almost fell off his back. A short spear shot past him, missing his left wing by inches. He resumed his course, and as he headed toward the armies on the ground, enemy archers loosed arrows in his direction. The dragon dodged them with ease and shot a stream of fire in response. His deadly breath had better aim, and many archers were engulfed in a bluish-green inferno. Belfynor exhaled again and hit a column of knights who were pressing down on the queen's warriors in the rear. He then turned around and scorched many wauld and dwarf battalions.

Belfynor opened his mouth to deliver another fiery assault when a particularly strong ogre in the enemy ranks took careful aim and hurled a long bronze pike at him. The weapon's pointed end tore into the dragon's chest and pierced his lung. He gave an involuntary belch, but nothing emerged from his mouth except gray smoke. Belfynor soon began to careen out of control. The celestonirs flying around him tried to grab his passengers, but he was moving too quickly.

"We're going to crash in the middle of Lord Evermore's army!" Belatro cried, pointing at the sea of soldiers below.

"Not if I can help it," Belfynor growled. With the last bit of his fading strength, he flew as far away from the enemy as possible and landed on his belly. The pike drove into his chest and out through his neck. When Christina was aground, she scrambled off Belfynor's back, her friends following, weapons drawn and ready to defend her against the ten thousand enemy soldiers rushing at them from the Well's northern side. Frantically shouting the dragon's name, Christina ran over to where his head lay. But she could see he was already dead. Caressing his snout, she let out heaving sobs. Meanwhile, enemy soldiers in the air attempted to reach Christina first and dove toward her exposed position, but the celestonirs, tree gnomes, and humans flying in the queen's sky force rallied to her defense and repulsed their attack.

"Your Majesty," Hymral said, putting a hand on Christina's shoulder, "A horde of Lord Evermore's soldiers are heading this way. We need to know what you intend to do. We can fly to the Well and attempt to place you into the portal, but we'll be greatly weakened without the dragon and our foot and cavalry force. However, if we return to our friends in the ground army, our fortunes may not be any better. They are completely surrounded, and Lord Evermore's soldiers are too many. Your other option is to order a retreat and escape to the Kaldewonn, where you'll be safe. We can attempt to reach the Well at a later time."

Tears of frustration stung Christina's eyes. Demoralized, she felt the urge to drink the Elixir and save what lives she could. But, determined to return home or die trying, she squelched this impulse.

"We'll head for the Well," she said, drawing her sword. "I'm tired of running away. It ends today. If I'm killed, sound a retreat and tell the others that I'm sorry for everything."

Hymral nodded. "It shall be done, Your Majesty."

"Let's go!" the queen shouted.

But before anyone could move, there came a musical blast from the direction opposite the oncoming enemy. Everyone, friend and foe alike, looked toward the source of the noise and saw an army of half a million miniatures approaching. Endless columns of glass knights on horseback led the way, followed by legions of infantrymen. The archers came next while artillerymen brought up the rear with catapults mounted on horse-drawn platforms. Sir Kranwick rode at the front of this shimmering army, and he held a long, thin horn in his right hand.

The Ifarthians were going to war!

CHAPTER THIRTY–ONE
THE FIGHT FOR THE WELL

Sir Kranwick rode up to Christina and said, "Good morning, Your Majesty!"

"What are you doing here?" she replied. "I mean it's great to see you and your countrymen, but I wasn't expecting this."

"Obviously. You didn't send for us, so we came anyway."

"But Raventir dispatched messengers throughout the kingdom to summon every loyal Imarian to my camp. Didn't any of them come to you?"

Sir Kranwick shook his head. "Like everyone else in Imar, they considered us to be of no use in battle. We thought you felt the same."

"No, I don't," Christina replied. "When you didn't show up, I assumed you and the rest of the Ifarthians were angry at me because you missed the battle at the Amber Castle. I thought you had decided to stay away or even join Lord Evermore."

The glass knight looked indignant. "We would never refuse to fight, nor would we side with your enemy. As soon as we heard about the upcoming battle against the Order, we made straightaway for the

Well Plain. All of us are here for *you*. You're the only ruler that overlooked our small stature and appreciated our martial virtues. It wasn't your fault that we missed the last battle. I hope we're not too late for this one."

"No, you're just in time," Christina replied.

After she quickly informed him of the situation, Sir Kranwick looked over at the approaching army and cried out, "Oh, this is the greatest day in the history of our people! Not only do we finally go to a battle, but we get to save the day! Your Majesty, my army and I shall help you reach the Well." He turned to his countrymen and shouted, "Archers! Ready your bows!"

The archers complied, and when Sir Kranwick gave the word, they loosed a volley into the sky. The tiny arrows glinted in the sun as they made their swift journey toward the approaching soldiers. When the arrows hit their target, the enemy reacted as if attacked by a swarm of bees. After ordering his archers to shoot at will, Sir Kranwick shouted, "Catapults away!"

Missiles the shape and size of large marbles, crystal balls, and short spears showered the enemy ranks, and legions of soldiers were bludgeoned or cut up in a grotesque manner. Those who could still use their legs started running toward the Well in a panicked throng.

"Cowards!" Sir Kranwick scoffed. "Let's show them how to die in an honorable fashion! Forth, Ifarthians! May your deeds inspire all true warriors from this moment till the end of time!"

He blew his horn again, and the glass knights charged at the enemy with the rest of their army in tow. Christina turned to the others, raised her sword, and shouted, "To the Well!"

"To the Well!!!" they replied in unison. Helvondir helped Christina climb onto the back of his peryton, and they launched into the air. Eelweed and Belatro mounted another peryton, and soon the queen's entire sky army was flying toward the Well.

***

In a short time, the glass knights reached the enemy's camp and passed endless rows of tents. The Imarians who performed the menial duties that allowed Lord Evermore's fighting forces to maintain their presence in the field fled when they saw the miniatures surging toward them. These humans and creatures had no wish to participate in a battle. The Ifarthians ignored them and continued their pursuit of the ten thousand fleeing soldiers. When the glass knights caught up with them, they slashed at their larger enemies with swords. The hapless soldiers didn't even attempt to defend themselves, and when they reached the Well, they ignored the Order's command to stand and fight and continued running from the battlefield.

When the glass knights clashed with the Order members, the latter stomped on their smaller foes, pulverized them with their weapons, or picked them up and threw them in the air. But the sheer numbers of glass cavalry brought down many of the Well's defenders. The Ifarthian infantry arrived soon and attacked in endless waves, and when the glass archers and artillerymen came within shooting range, their missiles rained upon the enemy. Things might have gone poorly for the Order if thousands of knights and infantrymen hadn't come to its aid. When Sir Kranwick saw the large knights and their horses, he raised his sword and cried out, "At last! Foes worthy of my glass! Forward, knights of Ifartheon! Let our enemy taste bitter death at the point of our swords! And if we perish on this golden field, then let him cut himself upon our shards! For Christina, Ifartheon, and Eternity! Aressindor, prepare our feasts!"

He and his fellow knights charged at the human cavalrymen, but the latter proved to be a formidable foe. Their plate armor and chainmail were impervious to most of the glass missiles, and their horses trampled on their tiny foes and kicked up clouds of dust and glass shards. But the tenacious Ifarthians slashed at the legs of the horses' tendons and brought many of them down, and the largest glass missiles knocked knights from their animals; once a human knight was aground, legions of miniatures finished him off. When the Ifarthian archers ran out of arrows, their comrades catapulted them into the air so they could land on enemy soldiers and attack them with swords and axes.

**

With great difficulty and perseverance, Christina's army in the sky fought its way to the area around the Well. When the queen saw piles of corpses and glass shards lying on the grass, nausea overcame her, and she nearly vomited. Despite their best efforts, her forces couldn't clear the contested ground, for thousands of enemy soldiers were entering the fight from the western and eastern sides of Lord Evermore's encampment, and her other army hadn't arrived.

Amidst the chaos of battle, an arrow struck Helvondir's peryton in the neck and caused the poor creature to crash-land on the plain below. Christina and Helvondir were thrown off his body by the force of the impact. The tree gnome quickly rose to his feet and rushed over to the queen.

"Are you hurt, Your Majesty?" he asked, helping her up.

"I don't think so," Christina replied. "How's your peryton?"

"Dead," Helvondir replied. "And the Well is too far away for us to reach without being noticed by the enemy. We must get back to the others."

But it was too late. Within seconds, several dozen dwarfs from the Order surrounded the two of them. Christina tried to pull her sword out, but Albrik grabbed her arms from behind. Helvondir reached for his weapons, only to discover that he'd lost them in the crash, and another dwarf pinned his arms to his sides. Gilfoit stood before them.

"Don't harm the queen!" he said to his comrades. "Lord Evermore wants me to bring the child to him so that he may kill her himself!"

Christina couldn't believe that her luck had turned this bad when she was so close to her goal. She decided to stall her captors in the hope of a rescue.

"Speaking of Lord Evermore, where is he?" she asked Gilfoit. "I haven't seen him on this battlefield. Is he a coward who lets others die for his own ends?"

This remark made Gilfoit froth at the mouth. "Don't you dare speak of my leader in that fashion, or I'll run you through!" he cried, brandishing his sword.

"Go ahead," Christina replied. "Then your precious leader won't get what he wants."

"Release the queen this instant, and you all might live to see the end of the day!" Helvondir said in desperation.

Their captors erupted in peals of malicious laughter.

"On second thought, Christina," Gilfoit said, "I think I'll kill you right now and tell Lord Evermore that you attacked me. The sight of your corpse should be enough to satisfy him." He stared at the ground for a moment before resuming eye contact with her, and his mouth twisted into a cruel smile. "How strange that you and I met at this very spot all those weeks ago. Once I sought to protect your life, and now I'm going to end it. Because of you, many of my friends in the Order are dead. But I shall avenge them right here and now."

As Gilfoit raised his sword to strike Christina in the heart, there came a swooshing sound. With a gargled gasp, the dwarf fell forward, a sword sticking out of his neck. Everyone looked to the source of the attack and saw Sir Owenday riding toward them. Christina cried out in relief at the sight of him but then saw that the knight was slumped over. One hand tried to cover a long, hideous gash on his stomach, and an arrow stuck out of his left breast. Several captors lifted their bows and prepared to shoot at him when Raventir and a dozen of her headless knights appeared.

"It's the enchantress of the Kaldewonn and her man-eating horse!" Albrik shrieked. "Run for your lives!"

He released Christina and tried to flee with his comrades, but a harpoon shot through the air, drove through the dwarf's burly neck, and killed him instantly. Startled, the queen looked up and saw

Eelweed and Belatro on their peryton. Meanwhile, Raventir and her knights quickly caught up with the rest of the captors and cut them down like stalks of grass.

Christina and Helvondir ran to Sir Owenday, but the knight fell off his horse before they could reach him, his bloodstained armor clanging as he hit the ground. Christina cried out in alarm. Kneeling over him, the pair gently rolled Sir Owenday over on his back. A few moments later, Raventir, Eelweed, and Belatro came over and dismounted from their beasts.

Christina turned toward the enchantress and cried out, "Help him! We can't let him die! Find Kellomeane and bring him here! He can heal Sir Owenday!"

Raventir shook her head. "I'm afraid Sir Owenday's wounds are too serious. He's not long for this world."

"No!" Christina shouted, unable to bear the loss of another close friend. "There's got to be *something* we can do!"

"Raventir is right," Sir Owenday said in a heavy, raspy voice. "Don't cry, child. I'm going to a better place."

"Maybe I can't save you, but you're not going to get me to stop crying," Christina said with a grimace as tears flowed down her cheeks. "I'm going to miss you, Sir Owenday. And I'm glad you came on this journey with me. You were the best bodyguard and friend anyone could hope for. Thank you for saving my life. And I'm real sorry I cost you yours."

"I'm not," the knight replied. "Even before I was cursed, I was never happy, for my heart was full of so much hatred and arrogance that it had no room for anything else. And after I was cursed, self-pity and despair was my lot. But your friendship changed all of that. And as I leave this world, I do so content in the knowledge that I gave everything for the sake of a beautiful and goodhearted child who caused me to feel joy for the first time in my life, helped me redeem my past wickedness, and taught me that a true knight doesn't require a horse."

Then Sir Owenday closed his eyes and died.

After Christina had a good cry, she turned to Raventir and asked, "What about the rest of our friends? Are any of them still alive?"

Before the enchantress could reply, there came a furious and familiar roar. Christina turned and saw Lord Bodwar, Charendaya, and Fryndain charge through a row of tents with waulds, polevicks, humans, and other allies following closely behind. There were several arrows sticking out of the bear's hide, but they seemed to have no effect on him. Spotting Christina, Lord Bodwar and Fryndain came over to her while the rest of the ground army attacked the enemy soldiers around the Well. After hugging them both, she looked at Lord Bodwar and asked, "Are you hurt badly?"

"I'm fine," he replied.

She turned to Fryndain and asked, "Where's Metorah?"

"Father was killed in the early moments of the battle," Fryndain said in a somber voice. "But he took many of the enemy with him. Don't be sad, Your Majesty. At this very moment, he is sitting at the great hall in Aressindor. And his sacrifice was not in vain, for your plan has worked."

"That's right," Lord Bodwar said, "And now if you'll pardon us, it's time to finish what we started."

He and Fryndain charged back into the fray while Raventir and a battalion of headless knights guarded Christina, Eelweed, and Belatro. Sensing that the battle was lost, thousands of Lord Evermore's soldiers surrendered or fled, and Christina's forces soon cleared the area around the Well.

The queen and her army had won.

CHAPTER THIRTY-TWO
FAREWELL

After the battle, the surviving soldiers collected the dead for burial and helped the wounded. Those among the enemy who surrendered were allowed to leave the plain unharmed. Except for Belfynor, Metorah, and Sir Owenday, all of Christina's friends emerged from the battle alive. The bodies of her dead companions lay side by side, and she kissed each one on the cheek.

Turning to Fryndain, Christina said, "Tell Erinonda that I'll never forget what Metorah did for me. My parents divorced when I was ten, and my dad moved away. I haven't heard from him since. But Metorah came all the way here and gave his life for me, even though we hadn't known each other for very long."

"Your father must be a fool," Fryndain replied. "How could anyone abandon their child? Shortly after you left our village, my mother and father told me that you were like a daughter to them."

"Thank you for telling me that," Christina said, wiping her face with her sleeve. "What's going to happen to your clan now that Metorah is gone?"

"I shall take father's place and lead with courage, fairness, and dignity, just as he did," Fryndain replied.

"You're going to make a wonderful clan chief," Christina said.

"Thank you. And you've made a wonderful queen."

Christina laughed. "I didn't rule for very long."

"The conduct of your reign is what matters, not its duration."

***

Christina didn't go into the Well right away. Instead, she watched as the bodies of ninety-nine Order members were thrown into a heap.

"Where's Lord Evermore?" she asked.

"No one saw him in the battle," Lord Bodwar replied. "Doubtless, he decided to let his soldiers and fellow Order members give their lives without risking his own. The Head of the Order has proven himself to be as big a coward as King James ever was."

When Christina was ready to leave, her friends and soldiers gathered around to say farewell. After thanking her army for its help, she embraced all of her larger friends before staring down at Sir Kranwick.

"Thank you," she said to the miniature knight. "We couldn't have won this victory without you and your countrymen."

"Thank *you*, Your Majesty," he replied. "Now we Ifarthians can enter Aressindor after we pass from this world."

"I'll never forget any of you," Christina said to her friends. "And I'll think about you every night."

"And we shall do the same," Raventir replied with a smile. The others nodded in agreement.

"Will you guys be alright after I destroy the Well?" the queen asked.

"Tomorrow, we shall all wake up to a much different land than the one we've known for thousands of years," Lord Bodwar replied. "But don't be concerned for us, Christina. Whatever the future holds, good or bad, we'll find some way to manage."

He turned into a man and plucked the arrows from his thick fur cloak before picking Christina up and placing her gently into the Well. As the golden water churned, she waved to the others, and they responded by cheering and shouting, "Long live Queen Christina!"

***

After the portal opened, Christina swam downward with the current as hard as she could. When she finally landed on the soft watery floor of the Room Between the Worlds, she scrambled to her feet. And gasped.

Standing not more than twenty feet away was Lord Evermore.

CHAPTER THIRTY-THREE
DUEL OF DESTINIES

"Hello, Christina," Lord Evermore said, a malicious smile imprinted on his broad weathered face.

"Boriandar!" she shouted, backing up against the wall. "I need your help!"

Lord Evermore laughed. "The Keeper can't hear you. He's in one of his deep slumbers. It's only the two of us. I'm going to kill you, Christina. Something I should have done a long time ago."

"How did you get in here?" she asked in an attempt to stall for time. This strategy had worked on the Well Plain, so it might work here. If she kept Lord Evermore talking long enough, maybe Boriandar would hear them and come to her rescue.

"Surely, you didn't think you were the only one who could open the portal, did you?" Lord Evermore replied. "My medallion grants me the ability to go to the Room Between the Worlds. As a matter of fact, I and the other Order members were inducted here eight thousand years ago."

"But how can you get back into the kingdom? You'll probably die in this room."

"After I kill you, I'll wait until Boriandar finds another child from the World Below and then escort that person to Imar," Lord Evermore said, pulling out his medallion and caressing it. "And thanks to this, I can wait for years. When the next ruler comes, there'll be no need for a quest. With no one available to take the throne immediately after your death, the kingdom will be thrown into chaos, and Imarians everywhere will curse your name. But when *I* arrive with the new child and set things aright, everyone will love me for it."

"How many children did you and the Order force into drinking the Elixir?"

Lord Evermore hesitated a moment before replying, "Everyone who came after Ethindir's death."

Christina gasped. "That's horrible!"

"We had no choice. There's something about the quest that makes the children desire to return to the World Below when it's over. It was different when Ethindir was alive. None of the children he brought to Imar had to destroy their predecessors since he did it for them. They simply drank the Elixir and took the throne."

"What would the great sorcerer think if he knew what you were doing?"

"Ethindir was a fool!" Lord Evermore spat, and Christina was surprised to hear the contempt in his voice. "I was his greatest disciple and the closest thing to a son he ever had, as he himself often acknowledged. But when I begged him to give *me* the Elixir and the Sword and vowed that I'd never betray their purposes, he refused, believing that no one from our world could rule forever without turning wicked.

And though the children from the World Below also went astray, he still gave them absolute power and immortality due to the longevity of their reigns. For the last eight thousand years, I've had to spend my life in a hole in the mountains and assist child after child in taking the throne. My leadership potential stifled, I'm nothing more than a servant, consigned to cleaning up after the messes made by the urchins from *your* world."

"If you wanted to rule, why didn't you just take the throne after Ethindir died and allow someone from my world to destroy the Well?" Christina asked.

"Ignorant child!" Lord Evermore scoffed. "If I had done *that*, I would have lost my immortality. And the kingdom and the Order would have turned against me, for most Imarians wanted the Cycle to continue, regardless of what Ethindir said. But I devised a plan after he rejected my request, and since then, I've bided my time and waited for the right moment to act."

"Where does the Prophecy fit into all of this? Did you really have that dream?"

Lord Evermore let out a cruel laugh.

"Even my fellow Order members don't know that the dream never occurred," he said. "The Prophecy is *the* essential part of my plan. You see, everyone assumes that it's referring to a child from the World Below. After another two thousand years has passed, when it is clear that the children from your world are really no different from the Imarian rulers of old, I shall reveal *myself* as the subject of the Prophecy, and everyone will believe me because of my long and devoted service to the kingdom."

"But if you become king, you won't be able to wield the power of the Sword of Etossar," Christina pointed out.

Lord Evermore shrugged. "I won't require it. My power will lie in my authority, and steps will be taken to ensure that no Imarian will attempt to seize the throne. And I will put the Elixir and the Sword where none can find them. When I have sat on the throne for a thousand years, my status as the Eternal Ruler will be sealed; I'll fulfill my prophecy. The Elixir will never darken, my reign will be everlasting and untainted by evil, and the Cycle will be broken forever. In the end, I shall become the ruler that Ethindir refused to be."

"What will you do with the children who travel up the Well?" Christina asked, dreading the answer she knew was coming.

"I shall keep the Well closely guarded at all times, and children foolish enough to come to my kingdom will be killed immediately," Lord Evermore replied, and there was a mad gleam in his eyes. "My rule shall rest upon their blood. They'll pay the price for Ethindir's folly just as surely as their predecessors did. And no one will weep for them because by the time *I* take the throne, all of Imar will have become thoroughly disenchanted with *your* kind."

"You're really sick, you know that?" Christina said, her fear now replaced by anger and disgust. "And you've been tainted by evil for eight thousand years. Even if you take the throne, you'll eventually be killed, like all the other rulers. And a child will find the Sword and the flask and destroy the Well after you're gone. Gil was wrong about you. You're not a great leader. You're a monster."

"Enough!" Lord Evermore cried, charging at her, his sword raised. Christina drew her own sword and met his attack. The two adversaries fought around the circular room, their dancing feet leaving furious ripples in their wake. Christina parried and thrust with all of the skill she had gained under Sir Owenday's tutelage, but in the end, she proved no match for her enemy and soon grew exhausted. With great ease, Lord Evermore knocked her sword out of her hands. Realizing that any further dueling was futile, Christina ran to the other side of the room.

"Silly girl!" Lord Evermore scoffed. "Did you really think you could defeat *me*? You can run around this room all day if you like, but you'll soon tire, and I shall catch you and finish you off."

Christina knew of only one thing she could do to save herself. While keeping an eye on her foe, she pulled the flask out of her bag, removed the stopper, and held it up to her lips.

Lord Evermore, advancing toward her, stopped when he was about five paces away. A smile spread over his face.

"Drink it," he cackled. "Summon the Sword and strike me down. But your soul will be bound to the Elixir, and I'll win in the end!"

He let out peals of maniacal laughter.

"If you want power that bad, then you can have it!" Christina said, pointing the flask at Lord Evermore's face. The geyser of Elixir shot into his open mouth, and he swallowed some of it before he realized what was happening. Dropping his sword, he clutched madly at his stomach and let out piercing shrieks that echoed around the room. Christina covered her ears to block out the noise but couldn't help watching with fascinated horror as a glowing white fire quickly spread across Lord Evermore's body, which soon dissolved into a pile of ashes.

CHAPTER THIRTY-FOUR
THE HERO WITH TEN THOUSAND FACES

After retrieving the sword and flask, Christina stared down at the golden floor, its beauty now marred by Lord Evermore's ashy remains. She was about to destroy the Well but then realized that Boriandar had neglected to tell her how.

"Boriandar!" she shouted. "Boriandar!"

Christina called for him until her voice grew hoarse, but the wellwight didn't appear. How long did his slumbers last? Maybe he wouldn't appear for hundreds of years! Boriandar had told her she could return to the kingdom if she drank the Elixir but doing so would condemn her to the very fate she had just escaped.

"No!" Christina cried out. "Lord Evermore isn't going to win! I won't drink the Elixir! *I won't!* I'll die here if I have to!"

In her frustration and anger, she threw the Sword and flask against the wall with all her might. They bounced against the reflecting stones and landed on the floor; the flask remained unblemished. Backing up against the wall, she sank down, covered her face with her arms, and wept softly. Christina couldn't believe she had been defeated by something so trivial. And after she had come so far.

A few moments later, she felt an icy draft and heard someone say, "Hello, again."

When Christina lifted her tear-stained face and saw the ancient wellwight, a wave of joy and relief swept away her despair.

"Boriandar!" she shouted. "Am I glad to see you!"

"Yes, it's me," the wellwight replied as he hovered in the air above her. "Who else did you expect?"

"Where have you been?" she demanded. "When I came down here, Lord Evermore tried to kill me. I called for help, but you didn't appear. You must be the heaviest sleeper in the universe."

"I haven't been sleeping," Boriandar replied, casually massaging his beard. "I couldn't assist you when you were in danger because Ethindir used powerful spells to ensure that I'd never interfere in the quest."

"I don't understand. I finished the quest several weeks ago when King James was killed."

Boriandar smiled. "That wasn't the quest I sent you on. I shall explain, but before I do, please relate everything that has happened to you since you entered the kingdom."

With the force and speed of a machine gun, Christina told him about the journey to the Sanctuary, meeting her friends, the battle at the Amber Castle, Gilfoit's betrayal and her imprisonment by the Order, the escape to the Kaldewonn Forest, and the battle on the Well Plain. When she finished with Lord Evermore's death, Boriandar beamed.

"Sounds like you've had quite an adventure," he said. "Now I shall inform you as to the real nature of your quest. When Ethindir realized that he would never find a child who could rule forever without succumbing to the corrupting influence of power, he concluded that all things, even great kingdoms, must come to an end."

"Then why did he create that stupid cycle?"

Boriandar held up a hand. "I'm coming to that," he replied. "Ethindir felt conflicted about continuing the process of royal succession. On the one hand, he disliked the idea that any more children should be destroyed by it—and, as I've mentioned, he felt that Imar wasn't meant to last forever. But on the other hand, he wanted the kingdom and its inhabitants to enjoy peace for as long as possible. So he established the Cycle to provide a great quest for the children of your world; the one who could go all the way to the Amber Castle, reject absolute power and immortality, and come all the way back here would succeed. None did, until now."

"But what about the Order? How does it fit into all of this?"

"Ethindir instructed its members to help children from the World Below destroy their predecessors, but—unbeknownst to them—their real purpose was to challenge those who accepted the quest. The great sorcerer knew that the Order would do whatever it took to keep the Cycle in place, despite his command that children be allowed to return home if they wished."

"How come you didn't tell me how to destroy the Well when I first came here? Was that part of the quest?"

Boriandar nodded. "I was forbidden from giving you that crucial information right away. In the unlikely event that you returned here, I was to see whether or not you would drink from the flask if you thought there was no other way out of this room. When you resolved to die rather than relinquish your soul to the Elixir, I was finally released from the confines of the reflecting stones. So congratulations, Christina. You've triumphed over the Elixir of Purity, the Sword of Etossar, and the Order of Ethindir. And now it's time for you to go home. Pick up the flask and lay it in the center of the floor. Then take the sword and drive it down the middle of the flask with all of your strength. The doors shall open and return you to your world and me to mine."

Christina did as she was told, and as soon as the sword struck the flask, they both shattered and dissolved. The water in the ceiling and floor began to swirl, and the wall burst into flames. Upon discovering that her faces in the reflecting stones were smiling at her, she smiled back at them. Then she turned to Boriandar and saw his chains appear. They glowed a fierce blue color and then evaporated.

"I'm free at last!" the wellwight shouted, soaring around the room. He flew over to Christina and gave her a hug. She shivered, for his arms and chest felt like ice. "Thank you, *thank you!*"

"Don't mention it," she said, strapping on her schoolbag. "I hope we can get out of here before this fire reaches us."

"Oh, we'll have plenty of time to escape," Boriandar assured her. "But when you reach your world, climb out of the Well as swiftly as you can." As the portals opened, he shook her hand and said, "Good luck, Christina. You succeeded where your predecessors failed, and both of us can now live a life free of the shackles of power!"

"Thank you," she replied. "Goodbye!"

Christina waved to the wellwight as he flew into the portal that led to Imar. Seconds later, she entered her own portal as the enchanted fire completed its destruction of the Room Between the Worlds.

Chapter Thirty-Five
Home

When Christina reached the World Below, she scrambled out of the Well and found herself in her special glade. It was nighttime, and the woods appeared empty of people. She looked around for her bike, but it was gone. By her own reckoning, she had spent at least a month in Imar and wondered how much time had passed in her own world. Now, she wore just her jeans, yellow blouse, and shoes. The clothes from Imar had disappeared during her journey through the portal.

She hid behind some trees and waited. After several seconds, a jet of white fire shot out of the Well and soared straight up into the sky, and when it came back down, the fire and the Well disappeared from the glade. Christina ran out of the woods and through the park and didn't stop until she reached her own neighborhood. Catching her breath, she stared with wonder at all of the houses standing shoulder to shoulder, with their green lawns, paved driveways, and two-door garages.

She was home.

Christina sprinted the final leg of her journey and soon reached her own house. When she came up to the front door, she was surprised to see that it was unlocked. After stepping inside, she closed the door behind her and even remembered to lock it. She ran into the kitchen, flung off her schoolbag, and shouted, "Mom! I'm home! Mom! Mom!"

Her mother flew down the stairs in her white pajamas, and Christina thought she looked like an angel in spite of her worn face and disheveled brown hair. Mom wrapped her daughter up in her arms and hugged her tightly. At the same time, Christina flung her arms around Mom's waist, and the two of them said nothing for a while. When they finally released each other, Christina said, "I'm sorry about the things I said to you the other day."

"I forgive you, sweetheart," Mom said, her face glistening with tears. "And I'm sorry for slapping you. But where have you been? I was afraid I'd never see you again."

"It's kind of a long story," Christina replied.

"Maybe we'd better sit down," Mom said. They went into the kitchen, and she made her daughter a cup of hot chocolate. When they were seated at the table, Christina asked, "How long was I away?"

"Two weeks," Mom replied. "When I woke up the morning after our fight and saw you were gone, I contacted the police immediately. I was sure you'd run away. They found your bike in the park, but nobody could locate any sign of you. I thought somebody had kidnapped you, and it scared me to death."

"I'm really sorry about that," Christina said. "I did run away. I meant to go see Dad but then decided against it and headed for home. Then something happened."

She paused, unsure of what to say next. Should she tell Mom the truth and risk looking like a liar or make up a plausible story? In the end, she decided on the truth.

"You won't believe this, but when I was biking through the woods, there was this magic well, and I got sucked in and—"

"Oh!" Mom interrupted, a stunned look on her face.

Christina didn't continue. She should have known Mom wouldn't believe her story. Who would? Feeling miserable, Christina waited for her mother to scold her for lying.

"Did this well have golden water inside it?" Mom asked in a quiet voice.

Now it was Christina's turn to look shocked. "Yes," she replied breathlessly. "But how did you know *that*?"

Mom smiled. "I think this well leads to a circular room with walls made of gemstones that show your reflection. And there's a wellwight named Boriandar who offers children the chance to travel to a magical kingdom and defeat an evil ruler. I should know; I was there once."

Christina sat in stunned silence for several seconds. "You were?" she finally managed to ask.

"My parents split up when I was about your age," Mom replied. "I lived with my mother, but she didn't really want me, and neither did my dad, so I ran away from home. I hadn't gone too far when that well appeared and swallowed me up. Boriandar offered me the quest, but I turned him down and went home because I was afraid of what was on the other side. You must be braver than me."

"No, I'm not," Christina said. "And you were right to stay here."

For the next hour, she told her mother all about her adventures in Imar and the friends who helped her return home. Mom listened attentively to Christina's tale, and when her daughter finished, she said, "Thank you for telling me that. If I'd gone to that kingdom, I probably wouldn't have returned, and I wouldn't have had you. You're dearer to me than a hundred kingdoms."

"So are you," Christina said. "And being a queen wasn't that great. You weren't missing anything."

"Listen, Christina, I have something to tell you," Mom said. "You'll like this. After you left, I had a talk with your father, and he has agreed to let you come live with him in California."

This news distressed Christina. "You don't want me to live with you?" she asked gloomily. "I guess I can't blame you after the way I acted."

"Oh no," Mom said, taking her daughter's hand and giving it a tender squeeze. "It's not like that at all. I *do* want you to live with me. I want that with all my heart, and I always have. But the one thing I want more is for you to be happy. And I know you've always wanted to be with your father."

"I don't want to live with Dad anymore," Christina said in a choking voice. "I want to live with *you*. Dad abandoned me, but you never did, even though I was horrible to you."

"I could never abandon you, sweetheart," Mom said. "You're my daughter, and I love you more than anything in the world."

"Even when I'm a jerk?"

Mom laughed. "Even then."

"I love you, too," Christina said, smiling. "And I'll never run away to a faraway land ever again. I've learned that life in this place is the greatest quest of all."

CHAPTER THIRTY-SIX
A WINTER SNOW

Christina stared at the millions of snowflakes falling outside her bedroom window as she waited for Sylvia and her mother to come pick her up for a sleepover. She loved watching a snowfall from the warmth and coziness of her home. These white crystals may not have contained any magic, but to Christina, they were magical nonetheless. Smiling, the girl reflected on her life and how fortunate she was.

It had been only eight months since she arrived back home, but everything had changed for the better. Shortly after returning to Grand Rapids, she phoned her father to let him know she was safe and that she wanted to live with Mom after all. Dad told Christina that her decision surprised him, but he accepted it and even invited her over for a visit. Reluctantly, she flew out to California to spend a weekend with him and his new girlfriend.

Christina immediately realized that Dad hadn't changed one bit. He was still the same selfish man who had cheated on and divorced his wife and abandoned his daughter. For her part, she made it clear she wasn't the spoiled, worshipping child that he remembered.

When Dad badmouthed his ex-wife, Christina stuck up for Mom and let him know she wouldn't tolerate that kind of talk in her presence. Although the visit proved to be an unpleasant one, she still went to great lengths to maintain a relationship with Dad. Having received the gift of unconditional love from her mother, Christina realized that she could give it others. And she grew closer to Mom with each passing day. Christina also kept her vow to try to be a better person…most of the time.

She also had her best friend back. Mom explained that during Christina's absence, Sylvia came to the house; she was sorry she had abandoned her friend in order to be popular in school and hoped Christina was all right. Shortly after returning home, Christina walked over to Sylvia's house, and the latter apologized for the way she acted. Christina forgave her freely, and the two of them became inseparable again. And Sylvia quit hanging around the popular girls—they bored her anyway.

Mom received a promotion at her job, and that meant Christina could spend her summers at the horse ranch. She made friends with some of the other girls there, and being with horses and nice children who shared her love of the animals only increased her happiness. She also packed away her books and medieval costume; she was through indulging in fantasies. But each night before going to sleep, Christina thought about Eelweed, Belatro, and the rest of her friends in Imar, and she knew they were thinking about her. And she often wondered what became of the kingdom after her departure.

***

When she spotted a car crawling up the snowy driveway, Christina pulled on her coat, grabbed her sleeping bag and pillow, and ran downstairs.

"Bye, mom!" she said, heading across the foyer.

Mom emerged from the kitchen. "Wait!" she called out. "Don't I get a hug?"

Christina immediately turned around and ran to her mother, and the two of them embraced.

"Do you need me to pick you up tomorrow?" Mom asked her daughter as they pulled away from each other.

"No, they'll give me a ride home."

"Alright." Mom smiled down at her. "Have a good time."

"I will," Christina said, turning back toward the door.

"Love you!" Mom called after her

"Love you more!" Christina replied. Once again, she forgot to shut the door when she went outside. Mom sighed and walked over to do it for her, but before she closed it, she looked affectionately upon her daughter as Christina ran out into the snow that descended upon the magical world.

The End

Acknowledgments

I would like to thank the following people for their help:

Author Anna D. Allen spent nearly two months poring over the manuscript and making hundreds of editorial suggestions—and her help didn't end there. Her constant support has been invaluable to this project.

Dr. Darrin Doyle (Ph.D.), professor of Literature and Creative Writing at Central Michigan University, taught me the craft of fiction writing and even took time out of his very busy schedule to critique my manuscript not once, not twice, but thrice. The amount of help he gave me was way beyond what I had a right to expect, and I will always be grateful for it.

Dr. James Smither (Ph.D.) of Grand Valley State University is a professor of History, not Creative Writing, but that didn't prevent him from providing essential help with this project. Not only did James critique the manuscript twice and offer helpful suggestions, he also answered a million questions about the Middle Ages and a host of other topics. His kindness (and patience) truly knows no bounds.

During the beginning stages of the writing of this novel, Dr. John Pfeiffer (Ph.D.), professor of Literature at Central Michigan University, was kind enough to do an independent study with me wherein he edited the very first draft of the manuscript, and his encouragement and enthusiasm provided a much-needed boost for a struggling new author. Dr. Pfeiffer also introduced me to Anna. His daughter, Rebecca, became the first member of my target audience to read the manuscript, and her glowing comments were another source of encouragement.

I would also like to thank Brian Rapp, Scott Stefanich, Rae Anne Beard, Bronwyn Mroz Benson, and Saul Lemerond for looking over various drafts. And a special mention should go to all of my former CMU classmates from the creative writing seminar for giving positive feedback on the first six (and admittedly bad) chapters of the original draft and convincing me to continue with a project that I had all but given up on.

And, lastly, I want to thank the highly talented Regina Doman for creating such a wonderful cover for this book.

About the Author

Born in South Korea, M.D. Couturier was raised in Michigan. Couturier, who is legally blind, once spent a month as an aid worker in Kabul, Afghanistan, where he unloaded supplies for an American dentist who was setting up a clinic there. *The Kingdom Beneath The Well* is his first novel. When he's not writing, Couturier enjoys reading history and watching movies.

Made in United States
North Haven, CT
08 July 2025

70471055R00134